Economic Regulation of the World´s Airlines

William E. O'Connor

Economic Regulation of the World's Airlines

A Political Analysis

Praeger Publishers New York Washington London

PRAEGER SPECIAL STUDIES IN INTERNATIONAL ECONOMICS AND DEVELOPMENT

PRAEGER PUBLISHERS
111 Fourth Avenue, New York, N.Y. 10003, U.S.A.
5, Cromwell Place, London S.W.7, England

Published in the United States of America in 1971
by Praeger Publishers, Inc.

© 1971 by William E. O'Connor

Library of Congress Catalog Card Number: 76-155217

Printed in the United States of America

International airline service has completed a half century of life during which the airplane has developed from an astonishing toy to a major instrument for the movement of people, cargo, and mail about the earth.

Governments quite properly attach large importance to international airline service and seek to protect and promote it. Many airlines are government-owned corporations, but all airlines, even though privately owned, operate under a mantle of governmental controls over both their safety and their economics to a degree far beyond that applied to most industries.

Yet, when one talks of the international, as opposed to the domestic, airline service, the familiar spectre arises of the inability of mankind properly to regulate the problems that technology has raised while we are divided politically into sovereign states. This study seeks to show that economic regulation of world airline service is essential, yet is hampered by an insufficient degree of international cooperation.

By contrast, the task of assuring the safe navigation of aircraft through the skies is characterized by a hearteningly high degree of practical cooperative endeavor among governments. But we will be concerned here strictly with economic matters--the right of an airline to establish service to another country, the control of the frequency of flights and capacity of aircraft, and the fares to be charged. This is an arena characterized by endless bilateral bargainings and a complex pattern of some 2,500 bilateral agreements.

This study explores possible changes in this method of economic regulation. In particular, attention will be paid to attempts over the years to substitute a multilateral agreement for the plethora of bilaterals. Two chapters analyze these efforts, and their failure over the quarter century since 1944.

Another chapter analyzes national and world aviation interests, broken down into political, psychological, and economic. This chapter suggests that the prestige concept, attaching great national pride to one's "flag" carrier, has become outmoded by the transformation of airlines from fascinating novelties to everyday servants; that economic goals should be broadened to dwell more heavily on the facilitation of world commerce and the promotion of the world economy. Similarly, it is suggested that governments have pursued narrow political goals of national advantage with insufficient thought for the contribution that international cooperation in this field of human intercourse might make toward goals of overriding importance, notably the reduction of international tensions and the development of a sense of world community.

The concluding chapter analyzes several systems of world economic airline regulation which have been proposed in the past and selects one of them, a draft agreement prepared by an international body in 1946, as the best choice. The "best system" is construed as that which will promote lower fares, centralize and simplify economic regulation, and contribute to two goals apart from aviation itself--the welfare and advancement of the less developed countries, and the lessening of international political tensions.

This "best system" would, however, involve so far-reaching a delegation of regulatory powers to an international body that it is unlikely that many governments would agree to it, at least in the immediately foreseeable future. Thus, a "second-best" system is suggested, derived from concepts in two draft multilateral conventions drawn up in 1947. These would leave the establishment of airline routes to bilateral negotiations, but in other respects augment the degree of international cooperation. As elsewhere in the study, the peculiar problems and interests of the less developed countries are given sympathetic attention.

Lastly, it is concluded that even if there can be no agreement among governments at the present time to change the "bilateral" mechanisms, it would be desirable to have a reorientation in the philosophy of airlines, governments, and peoples such that the world network of airlines would be seen less in terms of national advantage and more as a public trust for the peoples of the world.

This study was presented in 1970 as a doctoral dissertation at the School of International Studies of the American University in Washington, D.C. The assistance is gratefully acknowledged of the members of the dissertation committee: Dr. Durward V. Sandifer, its chairman; Dr. Mary E. Bradshaw; Dr. Warren S. Hunsberger; and Dr. Myles E. Robinson. Responsibility for any errors, as well as for all opinions herein, rests, of course, with the author. Moreover, since the author at the time of writing was an official of the Civil Aeronautics Board, it should be noted that the views expressed herein are entirely his personal ones.

CONTENTS

LIST OF TABLES

LIST OF ABBREVIATIONS

ECAC   European Civil Aviation Conference

IATA   International Air Transport Association

ICAO   International Civil Aviation Organization

ICATB   International Civil Air Transport Board (Proposed)

IMCO   Intergovernmental Maritime Consultative Organization

LDCs   Less Developed Countries

PICAO   Provisional International Civil Aviation Organization

Economic Regulation of the World's Airlines

1

This study will be an evaluation of the present method of economic regulation of the world's airlines and a consideration of alternatives. It will emphasize the broad goal of a world-wide system of frequent, safe, efficient, low-cost air transportation for passengers, cargo, and mail, on a scheduled basis, available to the peoples of the world. Yet it will have proper regard for problems going well beyond aviation, such as the plight of the less developed countries and the critical need for a reduction in international political tensions and the promotion of international cooperation. Thus, particular attention will be given to methods by which the economic regulation of world airline services might be reconstituted so as to make improved use of the practices of international administration. *

The current system is premised largely on a network of bilateral agreements. It can be criticized as tending to emphasize certain national interests, such as the promotion of the national airline as an end in itself or the use of civil aviation for the object of political prestige, while neglecting the world-wide public interest in having low-cost, efficient airline service without particular reference to the nationality of the airline. It can also be criticized for contributing to

---

*The term "economic regulation" may include the governing of one or more of the following: the right of entry--i. e., the right to establish service at a point--the route to be followed, the frequency of service, the size of the aircraft, and the fares to be charged.

international tensions by its emphasis on nationalistic state
policies.

In a sense, the problem might be cast in terms of economic nationalism akin to the high-tariff philosophy, contrasted
with a free-trade approach. Yet the matter is not that simple,
because airlines have some of the economic characteristics
of public utilities such as power and telephone companies, or
the rail or motor common carriers. An unreserved "free-
trade" approach, wherein governments freely admitted the
airlines of all other nations and placed no controls on establishment of scheduled services, quantity of service, or rates,
could result in destructive competition, chaotic service, and
the eventual elimination of rivals by the strongest airline,
which would thereafter enjoy a monopoly.

The economic characteristics of airline service (which
will shortly be delineated) are such that each airline feels compelled to reduce its fares to the level of any cut-rate competitor, with the result that a rate war can be particularly destructive. As will be seen, international rates rarely follow such
behavior in practice because they are controlled by governments and carrier conferences. Yet the consequent uniformity
of fares puts the airlines into a type of competition where the
passenger is attracted by the most modern aircraft and the
most frequent flights. As each competitor endeavors aggres-
sively to tap the passenger market to the maximum by frequent
services with a large up-to-date fleet, an excess of capacity
in a particular market can readily develop. These industry
problems will be developed in detail later in this study.

Many domestic airline systems are conducted by a state-
owned monopoly. The world system, however, has a limited
number of airlines in each city-pair market; the implications
of this situation will be considered herein.

Regulation by an international body (and perhaps by
regional bodies for regional services) has often been proposed,
but has thus far proved impossible to achieve. The specialized
agency of the United Nations--the International Civil Aviation
Organization--has extensive competence regarding the navigation of aircraft, and is a true regulatory body for the engi-
neering and safety aspects of world airline operations. But
is has no authority (other than the right to make studies and
recommendations) in the economic field.

This fact appears to reflect the grave necessity for world
safety and navigational standards, it being inconceivable that
the interrelated flight path networks could function, absent
such standards, without extensive confusion and an intolerable

level of aircraft accidents.   In the economic field, however,
it is possible (as experience to date has shown) to operate the
world's airlines without a central multilateral economic regulatory body, although this study will endeavor to show that the
lack of such a body has had undesirable effects.   Questions of
navigation and safety also tend to be less controversial than
economic questions such as what airline is to fly where and
what rates are to be charged.   Airlines, and the governments
that back them, are competitors in an economic sense, but
not with respect to navigation and safety.   Thus, it is not surprising that nations have been more willing to cede their prerogatives over navigation and safety matters to a world body
than to cede their prerogatives over economic matters.

Attempts to achieve multilateral economic regulation, if
not by an international body then at least by a multilateral
convention, have a long history.   The Chicago Conference of
1944 which established the International Civil Aviation Organization (ICAO) was the scene of an elaborate struggle, largely
between the United Kingdom and the United States, over the
nature and extent of such regulation, and there have been
several subsequent attempts to obtain a multilateral agreement.

The current system involves over 2,500 bilateral agreements.   Each of these grants to the other country the right to
have one or more of its airlines establish a scheduled service
into and out of one or more of the first country's cities.   The
route the airline will follow from its home country is usually
described, either by naming intermediate points or by use of
such general phrases as "via a reasonably direct route" or
"via a mid-Pacific route."   The agreement may also set forth
rules on such matters as the fares to be charged or the number
of flights permitted per week.   An airline flying a long international route, with many intermediate stops in different
countries, will find that a single flight may be governed by as
many bilateral agreements as there are countries on the route.

This study will begin by an analysis of the attempts to
achieve a multilateral agreement during the 1944-47 period,
the only time when this approach has received widespread
effort and attention.   This will be the subject of Chapter 2.

Later chapters will deal with subsequent efforts, including
the European regional experience and the one multilateral
agreement successfully negotiated and in effect today--that
governing intra-European nonscheduled flights.   The latter
constitutes the only practical success of the multilateral
method in the economic regulation of world airlines, albeit

limited to a fringe service and to one region. It raises the
possibility, which will be examined in later chapters, of a
worldwide multilateral agreement on such fringe services as
mail, cargo, or nonscheduled passenger flights as initial steps
toward broader agreement.

In the course of these analyses, certain widely accepted
concepts will be called into question, including (1) the assumption that having a national airline with international routes
gives a country prestige, and (2) the philosophy that a country
whose citizens furnish, say, 60 percent of the traffic over a
route is entitled to have its airlines carry that proportion of
the total traffic over that route.

Throughout, international airline service will be viewed
not as an end in itself but as a means toward world social,
political, and economic goals. Short-range political goals of
individual states, which often are factors in bilateral negotiations, will be contrasted with larger, long-range goals that
might be served if the economic regulation of the world's airlines could exemplify a high degree of international cooperation,
rather than the opposite.

The sheer newness of airlines--occupying, as they do, only
about the last fifty years of all human history--induces a vision
of goals radically different from anything previously known to
man. One such goal is already achieved: the movement of a
person (or of cargo) halfway around the earth in a matter of
hours, with consequent vast facilitation of the operation of the
world economy and of intellectual and cultural intercourse in
the world community.

But there is a companion goal that this new means of
transport has conspicuously not achieved: a sharply reduced
cost of travel. The price of air travel is generally comparable
to the cost of ocean travel, and thus the introduction of airline
service has made no substantial reduction in the cost of long-
distance international journeys. Many Americans cannot afford
to travel to Europe, South America, or the Far East, and many
others can afford to do so only on a "once-in-a-lifetime" basis.
And given the much lower living standards of most of the peoples
of the world, it is apparent that the great bulk of the human
race is for all practical purposes barred from any substantial
international travel.

There has been, to be sure, a considerable increase in
international travel in recent years, due both to rising living
standards and to the time-saving aspects of air transportation.
Thus, a businessman may travel to a distant foreign point
when he need take only a few days away from his job at home,

whereas before the advent of the airline he might well have
foregone the desirability of direct business contacts when he
could have achieved such contacts only through the much longer
time away from his job which ship travel demanded. The same
can be said of the worker with the customary two or three week
annual vacation. The time barrier has indeed been lowered
greatly, with consequent great increase in long-distance international travel, but such travel is still an expensive luxury for
most Americans and Europeans, and is virtually out of the
reach of most of humanity.

A round trip between the American East Coast and the
major European gateways, for example, costs over $400, al-
though, by using certain excursion fares (where one must return within a specified time, travel in an off-season, etc.) one
may obtain the service in a range of $250-$300. This is for
nothing more than transporting a person for about six hours
in each direction in a crowded cabin with a minimum of
amenities. By contrast, on an ocean vessel on a transatlantic
crossing, the carrier must feed and sleep its passengers for
a week in each direction, employing a crew on a round-the-
clock basis and a staff of food service and housekeeping personnel, as well as supplying such substantial amenities as
lounges and swimming pools.

Even at a rate of $300 on an excursion fare, the air pas-
senger is paying about $25 an <u>hour</u>. A tourist may well spend
more money for the two six-hour crossings than he will spend
for two or three weeks touring Europe.

Fares elsewhere tend to be even higher. At the present
writing, a round trip between the West Coast of the United
States and Australia costs about $1,000; between New York
and Australia the cost is $1,250. (An excursion fare is about
$250 lower, but is available only eight months of the year and
requires that the passenger return between two and four weeks
from his departure.) Added to the obvious economic and cultural burden this places on the world community, there is the
burden of its sheer inhumanity. Consider, for example, that
the "GI bride" from Australia of the Second World War may
never see her parents again, nor may they ever see her or
their grandchildren, though less than a day's journey separates
them.

The technology that has given the world such astonishing
speed might perhaps be asked to give it equally astonishing
economies.

Three particular economic characteristics of airline
operations should be kept in mind throughout this study since

they are central to the economic and regulatory problems.
Those are a largely undifferentiated product, a tendency to
monopoly or oligopoly, and relative ease of entrance.

Transportation by air is very much the same thing whether
one travels by one airline or another--i. e. , an undifferentiated
product is being offered. The highly sophisticated nature of
aircraft manufacturing has resulted in only a few giant firms
supplying virtually all the aircraft for the world's airlines,
with a close resemblance between one manufacturer's product
and another's in terms of speed, comfort, and safety. Though
the airlines struggle to create individual "images" in the public
mind, emphasizing such assets as French cuisine and Scandinavian stewardesses, it remains true that there is so little
differentiation that, for all practical purposes, the lowering
of a rate by one airline forces its competitors to drop to that
rate or face a massive loss of passengers. (In practice, as
will be seen, this does not necessarily result in any excellent
bargain for the passenger but, instead, in the setting of minimum rates by airline conferences with the approval of their
governments.)

As for the second characteristic, the airlines, as with
public utilities in general, exhibit a long-run tendency toward
the elimination of the weaker competitors so that, in the absence of regulation, only a few airlines, or only one, would
survive over a particular route. Many countries solve this
problem domestically by simply allowing only one airline to
exist, usually a government corporation. When such an airline ventures out on an international route, however, it cannot
escape the competition of the airlines of other countries. Yet
the monopolistic tendency is severely inhibited in international
aviation since each government will ordinarily insist on the
survival of its carrier and, to this end, will bulwark it against
economic forces by "protectionist" devices or by subsidies.

The third of the above-mentioned economic characteristics
may seem contradictory to the idea of the survival of one or
a few. Yet in an unregulated situation it is possible for an
individual or a small corporation to acquire one or a few aircraft and enter into competition with the giant airlines in a
manner that may give rise to an economic problem for the
latter. The airlines in this respect are comparable to bus
lines, but contrast with railroads. All three modes tend toward
survival of one or a few in an open competitive situation, but
the railroad must purchase its right of way and lay miles of
track before it can do anything at all, whereas the bus and
plane use public ways, and the small operator need purchase

only the vehicle.   Normally, he will compete with the giants
over their most heavily traveled routes, at cut rates which
he may be able to afford in the absence of any obligation to
serve leaner markets. *

There are other economic characteristics of airline
service which should be kept in mind throughout this study.
One is that airlines (particularly those with the long-range
services with which this study will be primarily concerned)
are moving gradually from a labor-intensive to a capital-
intensive condition. In the earlier days of the airlines, small
aircraft, relatively inexpensive to purchase but expensive to
operate per passenger mile, kept capital investment low compared to expenses for crews and other personnel such as ticket
clerks and baggage handlers. However, the trend in aircraft
has been to larger, faster equipment which is very much more
expensive to purchase but much less expensive to operate per
passenger mile.   (This is true for cargo as well as passenger
service; indeed, it was not until the advent of jet aircraft that
operating costs per ten-mile of freight became low enough to
permit fully self-supporting all-cargo scheduled services in
even the busiest markets.)

Two major steps along this particular road were the advent of jet aircraft in the late 1950's and the introduction of
the so-called jumbo jet aircraft, which can seat as many as
490 persons, which began in 1970.   The piston-engine aircraft used on the long-range routes of the world in the 1950's
cost in the general order of $1, 500, 000; the jet aircraft
in use during the 1960's on long-range routes cost about $6
million; the jumbo jet costs about $20 million.   Yet the more
expensive aircraft not only carry larger numbers of passengers
but carry them at a faster speed, and are therefore far more
efficient machines in the work of transportation.

In the transition from piston to jet in the late 1950's it was
found that the jet would carry twice as many passengers twice
as fast and so, in the course of a year, would perform four
times as many passenger miles. Although flight crews on the
jet aircraft receive somewhat higher wages, the number of
passenger miles per flight-crew hour was considerably greater

----

*In other respects this comparison would not hold true.
For example, if one were considering the carriage of cargo
in relation to the carriage of passengers, the airline is comparable to the railroad in that a single carrier handles both
classes of traffic, and contrasts with motor transport wherein
the bus line is a separate corporate entity from the motor truck
lines.

with the jets.   This must be multiplied again with the advent
of the jumbo aircraft, because although the latter are only
slightly faster than the conventional jets, they double the
passenger-carrying capacity with only a small increase in
crew wages.

The jet engine is expensive to manufacture but economical
to maintain and to overhaul.   This is another factor causing
the modern airline to move toward a condition where it can no
longer think of itself as having low "plant" investment, and
becomes instead an industry with a trend to decreasing operating costs per unit of service performed.

The constantly increasing emphasis on capital investment
gives the larger airline an advantage over its smaller competitor in addition to the advantage it already holds of being
able to schedule more frequent flights--it has strong leverage
with manufacturers to obtain early delivery on new types of
aircraft.   It has been found that the newest type of aircraft
invariably has strong passenger appeal.

The larger airline will ordinarily have cost advantages
over the smaller.   It will have the advantage of being able to
allocate aircraft and assign crews in accordance with the
varying, and often counterbalancing, demands of different
portions of its large route system.   Such costs as advertising
and counter personnel will ordinarily be averaged out over a
greater number of passenger miles, and the truly large airline can operate centralized maintenance and overhaul facilities.

It should be noted, however, that a very well managed
small airline may under certain circumstances operate a low-
cost service.   It may have a route system carefully limited
to its resources.   It may build with passengers a reputation
for efficiency and courtesy.   It may arrange with other airlines for pooled use of over-haul facilities and for the joint
ownership of so-called spare-parts pools which, in airline
parlance, goes well beyond small parts and may include such
highly expensive items as spare engines and spare navigational
equipment.

The usual economic concepts of supply and demand must
be applied with care to airline service.   In a superficial sense,
the supply of airline service is highly elastic since a specific
flight may be canceled or the frequency of service may be
reduced.   But, as a practical matter, an airline finds it a
competitive necessity to maintain its announced schedules and
maintain frequent departures.   Furthermore, to obtain and
retain qualified flight crews and to meet their usual union
requirements, it is necessary that they be on a year-round

salary basis, although they receive additional "flight pay"
which may be construed as a variable cost. With the trend toward aircraft with high original price, the depreciation on an
idle aircraft becomes a major expense. All in all, an airline
nowadays will find that if it does not utilize its fleet and crews
to the fullest, it will save very little on costs. In this sense
supply tends to be inelastic.

Furthermore, the acquisition of new aircraft requires
decisions to be made years in advance of the delivery of the
equipment. Thus an airline increases its "supply"--i. e., the
size of its fleet--in accordance with prospective increases in
traffic hoped for in future years. When aircraft are delivered,
supply jumps by sudden increments, and the airline may have
to face carrying many empty seats until the secular increase
in traffic which has characterized air transportation overtakes
the added capacity.

Supply is also affected by the seasonality of demand. As
will later be seen, the amount of passenger travel across the
Atlantic Ocean is far greater in summer than in other seasons,
and this is also true, though to a less extreme extent, in most
international airline markets. It becomes unavoidable that an
airline have an "oversupply" of facilities in the slack seasons;
it would be derelict in its responsibilities to the peak season
traffic if it did otherwise.

The question of elasticity of demand must also be approached selectively. A very small change in fare will have
negligible effect on the quantity of traffic, so that in this narrow
sense the demand can be described as inelastic. This argument is frequently advanced by airlines in objecting to small
fare reductions required by regulatory authorities. The reduction must be large enough to attract public attention and to
persuade a person to take a trip he would otherwise defer or
to use air when he would otherwise use another mode.

It is also true that the travel of businessmen tends to be
relatively price inelastic, particularly over the long international distances with which this study is concerned. The
airline offers such great advantages to the businessman, where
time is of maximum importance, that he is likely to fly without reference to the fare level. The tourist market, however,
is quite another matter. Here a substantial fare reduction has
been shown to cause a similarly great increase in traffic. For
example, when an excursion fare requiring a stay in Europe
of at least fourteen but not over twenty-one days (i. e., tied to
the prevailing practice of American vacations) was introduced
in 1964, offering a 21 percent cut from the regular economy-
class fare, there was an increase in travel that summer to

Europe of 25 percent. [1] Also, two more recent special fares,
both offering substantial savings, appear to have been largely
responsible for an increase of 17. 6 percent in passenger
traffic from the United States to Europe in the first full month
of their effectiveness (November, 1969) over the same month
in 1968. [2] Both fares are tailored to the tourist market: one
involves the purchase of seats in bulk lots by a tour operator,
the other is an excursion fare requiring a stay abroad of at
least four weeks.

The elasticity of demand in the tourist market when a
substantial fare reduction is offered is also demonstrated by
the history of charter flights, particularly across the Atlantic
Ocean. Charters of the type where the passengers contribute
to the flat price of the plane are required to be limited to
members of organizations existing for a purpose unrelated to
travel, and present other disadvantages such as the chance a
passenger may lose the entire prorated cost of his seat if for
some reason he is unable to make the trip or simply misses
his flight. Yet despite these disadvantages, and doubtless
because of the great monetary savings for the passenger,
charter traffic of this type represented about 15 percent of
all transatlantic airline travel in recent summer seasons.

The problems and dilemmas arising from these many
economic characteristics are, of course, compounded by the
political goals of the various countries and by the gap in technology between one country and another.

Even within the domestic airline system of the United
States, the economic characteristics cause problems enough.
To cope with them, an elaborate regulatory system was established by the Civil Aeronautics Act of 1938 which continues in
existence today under the successor legislation, the Federal
Aviation Act of 1958. [3] Entry into airline service is restricted
by a certification requirement, and a certificate for a route
will be issued only upon a finding by the Civil Aeronautics
Board, after public hearings, that the "public convenience
and necessity" require the service. Not only is the number
of airlines over each route thus determined by that Board,
but rates are regulated and strict controls are exercised over
mergers and interlocking relationships. The objective sought
is to limit competition on the one hand, and on the other hand,
to preserve it.

The American experience with domestic regulation is of
particular pertinance because there is a unique parallel between the American domestic system and the world system:
(1) the geographic expanse of the United States results in

long-haul services operationally comparable to the major
international (i. e. , intercontinental) flights, and (2) the United
States, unlike other large countries, has multiple domestic
airlines, generally comparable to the multiplicity of airlines
found on international routes. Obviously the parallel is not a
complete one, notably because the American domestic system
happily lacks the problem of separate sovereign states. Yet
since this study will be concerned with a possible regulatory
administration on an international level for the world system,
it will from time to time seek to draw lessons from the
American parallel. As will be seen, for example, fares within the United States are appreciably lower than for comparable
international trips. (There are, of course, certain higher
costs to be found in some international travel, such as higher
airport fees and fuel requirements for overwater hauls.)

A comparison of this sort was recently made by the
Secretary of Transportation of the United States. He noted
that an economy-class passenger between New York and Paris
pays a rate of 6. 4 cents a mile compared to 5. 6 cents for the
same class of service between New York and San Francisco,
although the former, being a longer trip, should be the cheaper
in light of the operating economies inherent in longer stages.
The Secretary further noted that the fare to points east of the
European gateways, such as Rome, are at an even higher per-
mile rate and that in the Pacific area, despite long staging
distances, "the lag between fares and operating economies is
greater yet. "[4]

A few words should be said here about terminology. Air
transportation has its particular jargon, which this study will
not employ any more than necessary. However, a few terms
will, of necessity, appear so frequently that they should be
clearly understood here at the outset.

The word "frequency" means the number of flights,
measured usually by the week, that an airline offers over a
route. The related term "capacity" refers not simply to the
number of seats (or tons of cargo-carrying ability) of the aircraft being used, but to this factor multiplied by the frequency.

Then there are the so-called Five Freedoms. This
terminology appears to have grown out of discussions among
the British Commonwealth countries prior to the Chicago
Conference. It is, of course, borrowed from the concept
of the "Four Freedoms" set forth by President Franklin D.
Roosevelt in the State of the Union Message in 1941: freedom
of speech and religion, freedom from want and fear. Although
it may seem something of an impertinance to have appropriated

for aviation the idea of enumerated "freedoms" from Roosevelt's famous statement, the terminology has become so much a part of daily intergovernmental negotiations on airline matters that it will be used in this study.

The first two of these Five Freedoms enter into this study only incidentally. The first is the right to fly across another country without landing. The second is the right to land in another country for refueling or repairs without offering any passenger or cargo service to or from that point. (This is a so-called technical stop, as distinguished from a "traffic stop.")

The Third Freedom is the right to offer airline service carrying traffic from the country of the airline's nationality to a point in another country. The Fourth Freedom is simply the opposite of the Third--i.e., traffic originating in the foreign country which is destined for the home country of the airline. In general, the two scarcely need to be differentiated, since the right to carry one nearly always automatically involves the right to carry the other. Possibly the two might have been combined into a single "freedom" except that in the early efforts to obtain a multilateral agreement there were some proposals put forward which looked upon the Third Freedom as being even more justifiable than the Fourth. In this study, there will be many times when these two freedoms will simply be combined as the Third/Fourth Freedom.

Lastly, the Fifth Freedom is the right to carry traffic which neither originated in, nor is destined for, the home country of the airline. An example of this would be Air France picking up a passenger in New York and taking him to Mexico City, or Pan American World Airways picking up a passenger in Paris and taking him to Rome. The great controversies in the 1944-47 era, and since, have turned more on the question of Fifth Freedom than on anything else.

It is important to note that the question of "freedoms" cannot be separated entirely from the concept of "capacity," any more than the concept "capacity" can be separated from the concept "frequency." As an example, a foreign government may be concerned about the capacity being offered by a United States airline into and out of one of its cities; this concern may be directed to the totality of competition being offered; however, it may instead be confined to the availability of seats for Fifth Freedom passengers.

It should be emphasized that a passenger is classified into a "freedom" category by reason of the origin and destination of his flight, and by the nationality of the airline, not

by the passenger's nationality.   An American in London, buying
a ticket there to fly to India, is Third Freedom on a British
airline, Fourth Freedom on an Indian airline, and Fifth Freedom on a French or United States airline. *

   With this brief mention of certain basic concepts of airline regulation, it is time to turn to the analysis of the attempts,
in 1944-47, to obtain a multilateral agreement.

                          NOTES

   1.   K. G. J. Pillai, The Air Net, (New York: Grossman
Publishers, 1969), p. 61.

   2.   Travel Weekly, (January 27, 1970), p. 1.

   3.   76 Stat. 143 (1962), 49 U. S. C. A. 1301-1542.

   4.   Address by Secretary John A. Volpe before the Inter-
allied Union, Paris, France, June 5, 1969 (United States
Department of Transportation Press Release 17-S-69), p. 5.

---

   *Ocean vessels, by contrast, escape the elaborate dwelling
upon "frequency," "capacity," and classification of traffic
which characterizes international air transport, and escape
also the whole requirement of bilateral route grants.   Instead,
through a combination of custom and general commercial
treaties, ocean vessels may enter and trade at any port.   See
John C. Cooper, The Right To Fly, (New York: Henry Holt
& Co. , 1947), pp. 127-9; David J. Padwa, "The Curriculum
of IMCO," International Organization, 14:525-6, 1960.

2

This analysis will be made from the standpoint of international cooperation versus nationalism, as indicated in the
previous chapter. Major attention will be focused on the International Civil Aviation Conference held in Chicago in 1944
(hereafter to be referred to simply as the "Chicago Conference"), since not only was this the landmark conference in
aviation history, but its deliberations remain even today the
most elaborate spelling out of the problems and conflicts be-
setting the economic regulation of international airlines.

This study will only be concerned, of course, with those
portions of the Chicago deliberations involving economic regulation. And the term "multilateral agreement" to be used herein
will refer only to a hoped-for agreement supplanting the bilateral agreements described above. The Chicago Conference,
of course, resulted in several multilateral agreements, including the basic treaty which established the International
Civil Aviation Organization, but the questions of routes,
capacity, Fifth Freedom, and rates dealt with in the bilateral
agreements were matters of the greatest conflict at Chicago
and remained unsettled at the Conference's end. The closest
thing to a "multilateral agreement" (in the sense herein)
coming out of Chicago was a proposed convention entitled the
International Air Transport Agreement, commonly known as
the "Five Freedoms Agreement"; only a few states accepted
it, several of these later denounced it, and it is today virtually
a dead letter.

In addition to Chicago, four other major events will be
dealt with in this chapter: (1) the Bermuda Agreement, (2)

the "1946 Draft" of a multilateral agreement, (3) the "1947
Draft, " and (4) the Geneva Conference of 1947.

The first of these was a bilateral agreement between the
United Kingdom and the United States, signed at Bermuda in
February, 1946, which, as will be seen, effected a working
compromise between the two signatories on routes, capacity,
Fifth Freedom, and rates, and has since served as a model
for many other bilateral agreements. (It is, in fact, contended by some that if the provisions of the numerous bilateral
agreements could be sufficiently standardized, the effect would
approach that of a single multilateral agreement.)

The 1946 and 1947 Drafts were proposed texts for a multilateral convention prepared by a committee of the interim
organization which subsequently became ICAO. The Geneva
Conference considered the 1947 Draft, endeavored to obtain
agreement, and failed.

THE REGIME PRIOR TO CHICAGO

Commercial scheduled airline service, other than a few
minor experimental ventures, began at the end of the First
World War, both in Europe and the United States. Since service
across the oceans was not established until the latter 1930's
(transpacific in 1936, transatlantic in 1939), there were nearly
two decades during which one network of air service was being
built in the Western Hemisphere and a separate one in the
Eastern Hemisphere. This is one reason why the principal
precursor of the Chicago agreements was largely a European
affair. It was the International Convention for Air Navigation,
signed in 1919, which was drafted by a Commission of the
Paris Peace Conference. This Convention (to be referred to
hereinafter as the "Paris Convention") established safety and
navigation regulations which governed European aviation until
Chicago.

For purposes of this study, the chief interest of the Paris
Convention is that it declared in sweeping terms the principle
of international law that a state has absolute sovereignty over
the airspace above its territory, and it made no grant of any
right to establish an international airline service. In short,
it left the establishment of world airlines to the bilateral bargaining procedure that still exists today.

It had one provision, to be sure, in its Article 15, which
could be interpreted as saying that once a state had opened an

airport for international use, it was obliged to admit to that
airport any airline of any state party to the Convention. In
other words, if a government allowed an airline of one state
to establish service at an airport, it thereby committed itself
to admit any and all airlines of all signatory states.

Such an interpretation, however, was not the accepted
one, and at a conference in 1929, Article 15 was amended to
make clear that a state was absolutely free to grant entry to
one airline and refuse it to another. It is interesting to note
that the United States (which, though it had not ratified the
Paris Convention, was invited to the 1929 conference) was in
the minority, along with the United Kingdom, the Netherlands,
and Sweden, concerning Article 15. These three governments
voted for the liberal interpretation described above. [1] What is
remarkable about this is that their positions fifteen years later
at Chicago were quite different and varied. In fact, as will
be later seen, the United Kingdom, the United States, and the
Netherlands came to typify three differing schools of thought.

Two other international agreements in the pre-Chicago
era should be briefly mentioned. The Madrid Convention of
Air Navigation, signed in 1926, was modeled on the Paris
Convention, but where the Paris regime tended largely to apply
to Europe, the Madrid sought to link Spain with Latin America.
However, so few states ratified it that it never became effective. The permanent administrative body it sought to establish never came into existence. [2]

The second agreement was the Pan American Convention
on Commercial Aviation, signed in 1928, commonly known
as the Havana Convention. Initiated by the United States, it
sought to do for the Western Hemisphere what the Paris Convention was doing for Europe--chiefly to provide uniform regulations for air navigation and safety. Like the Paris document,
it had a provision that could have been construed as a mutual
grant of the right to establish scheduled airline services. But
it was not so construed, and the rather extensive development
of airlines between the United States and Latin America in the
1930's took place via specific grants of rights either in agreements between two governments or, in many cases, in agreements between a government and an airline. [3]

The chief point to be made here concerning these three
conventions is that none of them relieved an airline of the
burden of obtaining traffic rights for each country along its
route through bargaining of some sort.

In consequence, there were numerous instances where
new airline services--some of them pioneering experiments

which technological advances had at last made possible--were
delayed. The British Government, for example, delayed the
grant of rights at Hong Kong and thus the establishment of the
first transpacific airline. The United States refused to grant
the Netherlands a right to have its airline serve between the
island of Curacao and Miami. The first transatlantic airline
services were delayed until the United States and the United
Kingdom were both ready to have their respective airlines
begin service, which at last occurred in 1939.[4]

During World War II, there was an intense expansion of
transatlantic air service, but although much of it was flown
by the crews and aircraft of the commercial airlines, the
service was under the administrative control of the military
authorities. These wartime arrangements had little bearing
on the willingness of governments to grant postwar commercial
rights. Their chief significance for the Chicago Conference
was the effect the operations themselves had on the American
and European vision of what postwar airlines might do. The
transport of men and cargo across the Atlantic, a tiny experimental service in 1939 when the war began, had become,
under the extraordinary pressure of wartime necessities, a
commonplace event. Furthermore, the expansion had included
service over difficult terrain. For example, there were air-
lifts to the Soviet Union which went far north of Norway (then
held by the Germans) into Soviet cities on the Arctic Ocean
such as Murmansk, and others which crossed the South Atlantic,
mid-Africa, and the Arabian deserts to Tehran. Similarly,
in the Pacific, large-scale air transport to the South Pacific
Islands, Australia, and New Zealand became commonplace.

The Chicago Conference opened November 1, 1944. By
that time, the European portion of the war seemed clearly in
its final phase. The delegates were meeting to design a plan
for the postwar world, and it was clear that the economic and
social importance of the world's airlines was to be vastly
greater than it had been in the two decades between the wars.
Moreover, there was a sense that the conference would tend
to set a standard for postwar settlements of economic problems
other than aviation where, as with aviation, strong commercial
rivalries would be involved. The work the conference was to
perform may be broken down roughly into four parts: (1) the
founding of a permanent international organization for civil
aviation, (2) the establishment of interim bodies to cope with
immediate postwar problems, (3) the regulation of safety and
navigational aspects, and (4) the regulation of economic aspects. The scope of the conference may be gauged from the

fact that fifty-four nations were represented and four hundred twenty delegates were accredited.

THE POSITIONS OF CERTAIN KEY STATES GOING INTO THE CHICAGO CONFERENCE

The United States Position

The American position, as presented at the opening of the Conference, was that routes should be the subject of bilateral negotiations, and that an international authority should be consultative only. The position was not specific regarding policies that should be adopted concerning frequencies, capacity, and grant of the several freedoms. It was stated, however, that airlines differed from ocean carriers and in many respects had economic characteristics more like those of railroads; and that it would be unfair to allow a newcomer to compete injuriously with an airline which had pioneered a service, except to the extent that the newcomer's traffic could be developed from Third/Fourth Freedom traffic.

As for rates, the United States, while opposed to regulation by an international authority, was "prepared to discuss ways and means" of regulating minimum rates.* Furthermore, subsidies by governments to airlines were held to be justifiable only "to keep planes in the air," not for "rate wars or uneconomic competition."[5] (The American position did not address itself to the difficult question of how such a distinction with respect to subsidies could be policed, but merely indicated that the United States was prepared to discuss the problem.)

Behind this formal statement lay about a year of discussion within the United States Government and with several other governments, notably the United Kingdom and Canada. It appears that at the first Quebec Conference in August, 1943, President Franklin Roosevelt and Prime Minister Winston Churchill had briefly discussed having an international conference on postwar civil air policy. Subsequently, the President made Assistant Secretary of State Adolf A. Berle the key

---

*Airline rate control frequently takes the form of regulating only the minimum rate, i.e., establishing a "floor." It should be remembered, of course, that since air travel is a nearly undifferentiated product, the lowest rate charged by a competing carrier tends to become the rate charged by all.

man in carrying out the President's wishes as to international aviation. Berle became Chairman of the United States delegation at Chicago, Chairman of the Conference, and the link between the President, on the one hand, and the Department of State and the Civil Aeronautics Board, on the other hand.

Although stated in general terms, the President's views seemed to favor a rather free exchange of rights. Indeed, in a conference he held with key American officials in November, 1943, a year before the Conference, he seemed to have favored an unlimited interchange of all five freedoms without need for route negotiations. This, at least, is what appears from Berle's memorandum of the meeting. [6]

However, this idea did not develop into a declared American policy. On the contrary, Berle advised the Canadian Government in March, 1944, and the Secretary of State advised the Chairman of two Senate committees in May of that year, that the American position would be to require bilateral negotiations for the commercial entry of airlines. Also, in June, a State Department official told the British Embassy that the United States did not agree that international airlines should operate under license from an international authority, and that it intended to proceed with bilateral arrangements. [7]

It was even argued in the course of the pre-Chicago preliminary work that any international economic regulation of airlines would be contrary to United States constitutional practice in the sense of being a delegation of regulatory powers to an international body. [8]

On the subject of frequencies and capacity, the position was less adamant.* Although "unlimited frequencies" were favored, the way was left open for a possible requirement that an airline justify an increase in frequency on the basis of specified high load factors over a specified length of time. As Berle phrased it in a conversation with the British shortly before the Conference: ". . . the increase in frequency would depend upon a fact" rather than upon a determination by an international body, although the latter might assist in ascertainment of load-factor data by being the recipient of periodic traffic reports from all airlines. [9]

---

*The United States, in its domestic sphere, has been able to leave decisions as to frequencies in the hands of airline management. In the international sphere, however, where a variety of airlines compete without a central regulatory body, subject to varying national policies (such as with respect to subsidies), frequencies are usually regulated, at least on an ex post facto basis.

It also appears, from pre-Chicago conversations with the British, that the United States favored achieving minimum rate control through an airline organization called an "operators' conference," a system similar to that employed by ship operators for many years. [10] Each government would have a right to intervene with respect to decisions of the "operators' conference," but the international authority would play no role other than to gather statistics. *

Defending its opposition to the grant of any real power to the international authority, the United States noted the pioneering activity of its citizens in aviation and the large predominance of American-origin traffic in international airline service. In certain discussions with the United Kingdom and Commonwealth country groups, it was noted that the United States "had originated 80 percent of all the interoceanic traffic" and that international control machinery would place a quarter century of American-developed aviation under "the unrestricted rule of an as yet undetermined international body, upon unstated standards." [11]

The American position thus advocated broad freedom in many respects but carefully withheld the most important thing that the United States had in its power to grant--the right to establish airline service to or from any United States point. It made the immense American traffic-generating power into a bargaining weapon through which it would obtain the most favorable world routes.

---

*Such an operators' conference was established shortly after the Chicago Conference as part of a carrier association known as the International Air Transport Association (IATA), to be discussed later. Its rate actions must be approved by the governments. In the operators' conference system for ocean carriers, rates are not subject to government approval and, moreover, the governments do not have (as a practical matter) the right to bar entry of a carrier for charging a rate they do not like, inasmuch as there is virtual freedom of entry for ocean shipping. (See footnote, Chapter I, p. 15.) Governments do, however, seek to regulate ocean shipping by subsidy policy and by cargo preference and similar laws. In turn, maritime operators' conferences have resisted these indirect governmental controls by devices such as reducing services and raising rates. The conference operators also have the device of the "fighting ship" which matches the sailing schedule of non-conference competitors and undercuts the latters' rates, with its losses covered by the conference members.

It is a reasonable economic argument that free competition
by airlines whereby they would make their own managerial
decisions as to frequency, capacity, and, to some extent,
rates, is an arrangement ultimately beneficial to the consumer
in the sense of letting him, by his choice of airline, determine
which line would profit and expand. By contrast, however,
the granting of airline routes premised on the national origin
of the traffic has a political rather than an economic basis.
Under such a system, the United States airlines would be assured elaborate routes throughout the world, regardless of
efficiency or passenger preference. Furthermore, a foreign
government might have to accept rights at secondary American
points in return for admitting United States carriers to its
major cities.

This seems a pure example of nationalism overriding
economics. It is as if a passenger were somehow a bargaining
pawn to the government of the country where he purchases his
ticket.

The Position of Australia and New Zealand

The position of Australia and New Zealand was a joint
one and will be mentioned here since it is, in a sense, at the
opposite extreme to the American position.

Where the United States envisioned that virtually no power
over economic matters would be vested in an international
authority, Australia and New Zealand proposed that such an
authority should actually operate the major trunk routes of the
world. This authority would be an organ of the United Nations
Organization which, at the time, had been delineated at the
Dumbarton Oaks meeting but had yet to be established. It
would actually own the aircraft and carry on the full managerial
function. Each country, however, would be free not only to
have whatever regime it chose for its domestic services but
to establish services through bilateral arrangements with contiguous and nearby nations. Thus, the United States would
have service to Canada by American and Canadian airlines,
to Guatemala by American and Guatemalan carriers, but
would have service to Europe, the Far East, and South America
exclusively via the international carrier.

In defending this proposal, the delegate of New Zealand
stated that:

> . . . any other system, we suggest, leads to
> national competition, to an attempt to serve

national interests as against world interests, to
achieve individual needs at the expense of others.
It must lead to the creation and expansion of large
commercial organizations whose activities must in
the long run be based primarily on the profit motive.
It may well be felt that in commercial hands there
might be some small degree of extra efficiency; I
would ask you to balance this possibility with what
seems to us the certainty of a commercial and
national rivalry in this field which must lead in the
long run to commercial and national competition
and ill-will, and which cannot in the long run hope
to achieve that proper balance between the rights
and the necessities of all nations, which would to
a much greater degree be within the competence
of an international body. [12]

To this, the Australian delegate added that there would
be an advantage in having one international authority conduct
all world services since such an authority "would have at its
command all the best technical, research, and other aviation
resources of all countries. Under past conditions such resources were often preserved in secrecy in national interests,
instead of being pooled in the common interests of mankind. "[13]
    Although this was the formal position of the two countries
when the Chicago Conference opened, it is clear that they
already realized that their proposal was not going to be accepted. They were prepared to accept something more along
the lines of the Canadian and United Kingdom positions which,
as will subsequently be seen, would have left the airlines under
national flags but with an international authority holding strong
regulatory powers over them. [14]
    The fate of the proposal at Chicago was to be quickly dis-
missed from serious consideration, and the two Commonwealth
countries devoted their efforts to supporting the Canadian and
United Kingdom positions. It seems pertinent, however, to
quote here a comment made a year after the conference to the
effect that the New Zealand-Australian concept "might have
meant great advantages for the ordinary traveller who worries
very little about the politics behind his flight, just so he gets
there. " The same writer went on to declare:

    It could have meant larger and more comfort-
    able planes on all routes, since one company could
    gauge the flow of traffic with greater accuracy.

But the two little English-speaking nations from
down under got a quick brush-off. Certainly both
the United States and the United Kingdom acted as
if the family pup had dragged a dirty shirt into a
formal tea party. [15]

The arguments against the proposal were practical political
ones. They can best be summarized in the words of a leading
Netherlands expert in air law, Dr. D. Goedhuis, who some
two and a half years after the conference referred to the single
airline proposal in these terms:

The essential and, in my opinion, insuperable
objection to plans of such a nature lies in the fact
that the international aviation problem constitutes
a part of the universal political problem of world
organization, and that the former cannot be solved
independently of the latter. It is an idle dream to
believe that the states will be prepared to entrust
to an international organization such an important
economic and political attribute of power as aviation so long as they are not inclined to greater
cooperation on wider political terrain. [16]

Parenthetically, it should be noted that the Labour Party
in the United Kingdom favored a single international airline.
Since it was not in power at the time of Chicago, its position
was not that of the United Kingdom Government. Its arguments
emphasized security, and clearly were influenced by the recent British experience with bombardment by German aircraft; it held that protection from the antisocial use of aviation
required that civil flying be put under the actual ownership
and operation of a world authority. The Labour Party also
contended that the development of air transportation prior to
the war had been disappointing, whereas the great pooling of
military air power (i.e., in a sense, its "internationalization")
during the war had resulted in greatly enhanced efficiency and
technical progress. [17]

The Position of Canada

Perhaps the most detailed and thoughtful proposal to be
put before the Conference was Canada's. It envisaged an
international authority modeled closely on the Civil Aeronautics

Board of the United States. In order to operate an international
route, an airline would have to obtain a certificate from the
authority which would not only describe the route but would
specify the initial frequency and rates. Issuance of the certificate would automatically give the airline the right to operate
the route on the basis of the first four Freedoms. With respect
to Fifth Freedom, however, the Canadian proposal deviated
from the international-authority concept and made a sharp
concession to bilateralism. Fifth Freedom rights could not
be granted by the authority, but could be obtained only by bilateral negotiations between the airline's government and the
governments along its route.

The authority would have consisted of twelve members,
eight designated by the major air powers, four elected by the
Assembly of the international aviation organization which the
Conference was to create. There would also have been regional councils, each of which would act with the same powers
as the central authority when a route was wholly within its
region.

Standards were to be set forth for both the international
authority and the regional councils to follow. Routes and
services, for example, were to be "fairly and equitably" dis-
tributed among states in accordance with their needs for air
service and their "industrial and scientific resources," but
attention was also to be given to the needs of the users of
airlines for safe, economical air transportation. [18]

What was to become a major issue at the Conference was
the so-called escalator clause which the Canadians advanced.
This prescribed the standard by which the authority was to
grant an airline an increase in frequency above that granted
in its certificate. If a route were operated for twelve months
with an average load factor of at least 65 percent, the authority
would permit an increase in frequency. If the average load
factor ran below 40 percent over a twelve-month period, the
authority could direct a reduction in frequency, provided that
there could be no reduction below one weekly round trip for
one airline of every state on every route which began in that
state's territory.

The authority was to be obliged to permit any state to
operate one airline from its own territory to any and every
point on earth, but subject to the severe limitation to one round
trip a week. Obviously it would normally certificate a new
service, in its discretion, for a much higher level than this
token service. But the basic right to the token service was
not merely a concession to nationalism; it was also intended

to keep the door open for the small or new airline of a small
state to win itself a higher frequency allotment, via the escalator clause, by demonstrated passenger preference.

As for the regulation of rates, the airlines would be required to file tariffs with their regional councils; any government would have the right to file objections; the regional
council would then hold hearings and would have the right to
modify the tariff. The standard to be followed by the regional
council would be that a rate should be set so that the lowest-
cost operator over the route would cover the full cost and obtain a reasonable profit. A decision by a regional council
could be appealed to the central authority.

The foregoing Canadian position presented to the Conference was substantially the same as that which Canada had
earlier submitted informally to the United States, the United
Kingdom, and the British Commonwealth countries in March,
1944. There had followed that spring some exploratory discussions between Canada and the United States in Montreal
which served largely to demonstrate to both countries the
great difference in their views. [19]

The Position of the United Kingdom

The British position was less definite than those previously
discussed. There had been a position taken privately with the
United States which had consisted first of backing the Canadian
proposal and then of receding, again privately, to the position
where the question of the powers to be allocated to the international authority was left carefully open. [20]

The position presented at the Conference was that of a
White Paper that had been submitted to Parliament the previous
month by the Secretary of State for Air. [21] It advocated that
"freedom of the air should extend" to the first four Freedoms,
with Fifth Freedom "a matter for negotiation." It appeared
to favor an international authority along Canadian lines with
power to issue licenses and determine rates and frequencies.
Yet it concluded by carefully opening the way for changes.
Its final sentence reads: "The proposals are of a provisional
nature and may be modified in the light of views expressed by
other countries."

Light is shed on the true British position in a telegram
sent by Adolf A. Berle to the Department of State on April 7,
1944, when he was in London carrying on preliminary discussions. Berle begins to the effect that: "A crisis developed

in our aviation discussions because of insistence of the British on ironclad international economic as well as technical control of international aviation." However, later in the same telegram appears the following interesting account of the entrance of Prime Minister Churchill personally into the problem:

> At this stage in the conversations (noon April 6) Beaverbrook and I went over to lunch with the Prime Minister. Beaverbrook reported on the general situation and our divergences over the British desire for international control. I pointed out our constitutional and political difficulties. The Prime Minister dealt rather lightly with the whole internationalized thesis saying that he considered the heart of any agreement finally reached would have to be understanding between the British and the United States, and he then and there instructed Lord Beaverbrook not to press the extreme position and in any event to arrive at an agreement. My private opinion is that the British never really intended to press for complete international control of aviation but made the contention for the benefit of certain members of the British Cabinet who have taken advanced public positions in favor of internationalism not only in aviation but in general. [22]

That Berle correctly interpreted the Prime Minister's position seemed confirmed later when, on July 21, 1944, he reported to the Department of State as follows:

> At lunch with Lord Beaverbrook today, he gave his ideas as to the possible course of civil aviation matters. He said that he was under instructions to maintain the desire for a strong international body which could regulate civil aviation matters. He was fully aware of our position, which was that we could not assent to this. I gathered, however, from the conversation that at an appropriate time the British Government will recede from its position. Lord Beaverbrook, indeed, indicated that there would have to be several days battle at an international conference before this would be achieved. [23]

As will shortly be seen, the British delegation did partly as Berle had anticipated--i.e., receded from the concept of

an international authority with strong regulatory powers. Yet
the British continued to favor an "internationalized" system
in the sense of controls on frequency, capacity, and Fifth
Freedom to be written as formulas into a multilateral agreement.

The Position of the Soviet Union

The Soviet Union intially accepted the invitation to Chicago,
but at the last minute announced that it would not attend because
of the fact that three countries--Portugal, Spain, and Switzer-
land--would be present.   These three were neutral in the
Second World War, although in the case of Spain the "neutrality"
had been definitely slanted toward the Axis side. Spain had
sent forces to fight beside the Germans on the Russian front,
and this fact was noted in the Soviet announcement.

Thus there was no Soviet position presented at the Conference.   There had been discussions, however, between the
Soviet Union and both the United States and the United Kingdom
in the late spring of 1944, including a visit of Soviet aviation
experts to the United States. Out of these discussions had
come a definite Soviet position.

It was that all international air service into and out of
Soviet territory was to be carried by Soviet aircraft, but that
the airlines of other countries might connect with the Soviet
airline at agreed points. A specific example which a Soviet
representative gave to Adolf Berle was a service between the
United States and Moscow wherein an American airline would
carry traffic as far as Cairo where the Soviet airline would
pick it up. It was, however, indicated by Soviet officials that
there was at least a possibility of admitting a foreign airline
to a gateway city in the Soviet Union where the transfer to the
Soviet airline would take place.

Berle's recommendation within the Department of State
was that the United States should proceed to seek relatively
open communications for airlines throughout the world even
though it appeared that the Soviet Union would not participate
in this policy and would choose to remain "as a great closed
enclave. "[24]

Despite remonstrances by the United States, the Soviet
Government insisted on its refusal to attend the Conference,
and declined even to permit Soviet aviation experts, who by
that time had already arrived in the United States, to sit as
observers for purposes of liaison. [25]

Its absence from Chicago, while it undoubtedly simplified the job of obtaining agreement both on the navigational and economic aspects of aviation, nevertheless left the great expanse of Soviet territory outside the world's civil aviation regime. This was of little immediate moment during the early years after the war when the Soviet Government permitted no foreign aircraft to enter its airspace. As time went on, however, certain Western European airlines were permitted to conduct regular airline service to Moscow. More recently, in 1968, after long negotiations, the Soviet Union has admitted the American airline, Pan American World Airways, to Moscow, and the United States has admitted the Soviet carrier, Aeroflot, to New York.

The Soviet Union thus now has airlines in the world network yet remains outside ICAO.* In matters of navigation, it follows of necessity the standards set by ICAO without having any say in setting them. In economic matters, it negotiates bilateral agreements in the same manner as other countries.

THE NEAR-AGREEMENT OF THE KEY
COUNTRIES AT CHICAGO

Probably the closest the world has ever come to obtaining a truly internationalized regime of civil aviation occurred near the end of the Chicago Conference when the United States and United Kingdom, with Canada acting as mediator, came close to agreement. The elaborate negotiating steps by which the two major air powers approached what might have proved an acceptable compromise will not be detailed here. Instead, the positions of the two states at the point nearest agreement will be analyzed, as will the final (but unaccepted) compromise which Canada advanced.

Agreement was reached that the international authority would have powers limited strictly by formulas, to be written into the multilateral agreement, for the regulation of capacity and Fifth Freedom, that the signatory governments would be obliged to observe. The ultimate disagreement came on the question of whether there would be an escalator with respect to Fifth Freedom. The British were prepared to accept an

_____

*Since the above was written, the Soviet Union has adhered to the Chicago Convention and become a member of ICAO, effective November 14, 1970.

escalator when the load factor of Third/Fourth Freedom traffic averaged above an agreed percentage. The United States, however, insisted that there also be permissible increases of frequencies based on a load factor which included Fifth-Freedom traffic.

This may at first seem a rather nice point. In practice, however, the British plan would have meant that American airlines would have had difficulty justifying increases in capacity on services beyond the Western European gateways. Such services might have been held indefinitely to the initial token minimum of one round trip a week. The British, on the other hand, felt that if American airlines were allowed to justify capacity increases based on traffic with no relation to the United States (e.g., Britishers traveling from London to India or Frenchmen traveling from Paris to Cairo), there would be no limitation on the expansion of United States airline services, and they would drive competitors out of the air.

The discussion to follow will cover this matter in much detail since it is critical to an understanding of how the world might have arrived at something approximating an international regulation of airlines. This will include portions of the personal messages exchanged between Roosevelt and Churchill wherein the sharp issue of the application of the escalator clause to Fifth Freedom was recognized but where agreement could not be reached.

The "ultimate" United Kingdom position was set forth in Conference Document 384. [26] The "ultimate" United States position was to be found in Document 385. [27] The Canadian draft language of the crucial article (Article XI) appears as Document 407. [28] Both the United States and the United Kingdom refused to accept the middle position proposed by Canada, and the Chicago Conference at that point gave up trying to get agreement on this whole matter.

The Three Documents

Powers of the International Authority

Where the initial United Kingdom and Canadian proposals to the Conference had been to require that an airline obtain a certificate from the international authority before it could begin to operate on an international route, the three documents herein agreed that the authority would have no such far-reaching powers. Instead, any country could unilaterally establish a

route to any other country and get beyond to further countries,
the only limiting requirement being that its airline must follow
a "reasonably direct" routing.

A route, of course, would have to begin in the home country
of the airline; there would be no right, for example, for an
American airline to establish a route which merely ran between Australia and New Zealand. Yet it would be permissible
for any airline to establish even a round-the-world service.
The amount of service that could be established on such a
route, and the type of traffic which could be picked up were,
however, quite another matter.

Permissible Capacity

The three documents agreed that the airline, upon departure from its home origin point, would be entitled to establish capacity equal to 50 percent of that necessary to carry all
traffic originating in its home country and traveling to the
various countries along the route. (This would all be Third
Freedom traffic.) The three also agreed that a minimum
capacity of one round trip a week over a route was permissible without regard to the 50 percent standard. In short, all
were agreed that a country could have its airline begin a
service from its home territory to any signatory state on the
basis of this minimum token frequency, and endeavor to build
up its traffic so as to justify later increases.

Here, and throughout this chapter, a capacity capable of
carrying 50 percent (or other percentage) of the traffic between two points means a capacity capable of carrying such
traffic at an average load factor of 60 or 65 percent. Furthermore, the average would be computed over a full year, so
that seasonal traffic fluctuations would be allowed for. In effect, it was assumed that an airline's aircraft were in a sense
running "full" if 60 or 65 percent of the seats averaged filled.
(The Conference never decided whether 60 or 65 should be
the accepted level.)

Fifth Freedom and the Escalator

Once an airline has stopped at its first foreign point, the
critical question arises as to how much capacity it may offer
to points beyond. For example, a United States airline flying
New York-London-Paris-Rome-Cairo, with no right to pick
up Fifth Freedom, would experience a gradual emptying of
the plane as it progressed through the European points, with

the plane nearly empty on the average final leg into Cairo.
Not only would this be highly uneconomic for the airline, but
it would involve the irrational act of having to refuse passengers
at London who wished to travel to Cairo even though empty
seats were available.

The airline, denied Fifth Freedom, could, of course, be
told to resolve its problem by reducing the size of its aircraft
as it proceeds from city to city. (For this, the airline jargon,
borrowed from the railroads, is "change of gauge.") One
obvious objection to this is that through passengers will be
put to the inconvenience of having to change to the smaller
aircraft at each point. Another is that fleets of aircraft would
have to be maintained at each foreign point.

The more likely adjustment would be to reduce frequency
at each foreign point. There might, for example, be three
daily trips out of New York, one of which would terminate at
London and another at Paris, so that only one trip each day
would go on to Rome and perhaps only a trip on alternate days
would continue to Cairo. This may sound reasonable enough,
but in practice it can raise serious problems. An airline passenger desiring to travel to Cairo will very likely wish to
travel on a specific date; if an airline does not have a flight
on that date, he will travel on a different airline. Thus, running the trip through to Cairo on alternate days of the week
rather than on every day may help little with the economics
of that last leg of the route.

This phenomenon is less serious where there is a daily
flight, but even then a passenger wanting a morning departure
will be very unlikely to wait until evening to depart on a particular airline when he can obtain a morning departure on a competitor. This is one basic dilemma in trying to plan transportation of any sort: frequencies should be adjusted to the amount
of traffic available, but the amount of traffic available will
depend partly on the frequencies.

The United States, of course, wanted to leave an airline
wholly free to determine its frequencies and to carry all the
Fifth Freedom traffic it could attract. It had agreed, however, as has been stated above, that when service was first
initiated over a route, the capacity on departure from the home
country would be limited to half of that necessary to carry all
air traffic proceeding from the home country to all countries
on the route, as determined by the international authority.*

---

*In Document 385, the U.S. Delegation stated that it "ex-
pressly does not commit itself to these proposals at this time

From the first foreign point onward, however, a very complicated method was to be used for determining how capacity should be "shrunk" as the route progressed away from the home country, on this initial service, as follows:

1. A system of "sectors" and "divisions" would be established. A "sector" was defined simply as a segment flown nonstop between any two points. A "division" was defined as that portion of a route where the capacity of an airline is uniform. One goes, that is to say, from one division to the next at that foreign point along the route where certain of the airline's flights terminate, while others go on.

2. The airline could maintain capacity from point to point along the route without being open to challenge before the International Authority, provided that it shrank capacity according to the formula that Third Freedom traffic over the last sector of a division would have to be at least 50 percent of that moving over the first sector of that division. To use the New York-Cairo example again, if more than half the passengers, on average, were disembarking at London, then New York-London would have to be called a "division" and frequency would have to be reduced at London.

3. An airline might, however, choose to initiate service over a route with capacity higher than the above-described level, using anticipated Fifth Freedom traffic as justification. But in such an event the International Authority could review the matter and "recommend an adjustment. "*

After one year of operation, the airline could apply an escalator which would give it rather broad rights to increase capacity. Thus, it could increase capacity along the entire route if the load factor over the year had averaged more than 65 percent over any one segment of the route in either direction. (The language used, and so defined, is "the critical operational

---

but puts them forward for study and suggestion in an effort to set up a basis for discussion looking toward the evolution of a generally acceptable proposal. " However, since the proposals were nevertheless formally set forth in a Conference Document, they will be used herein as representative of the furthest extent to which the U. S. was apparently prepared to go.

*"Recommend" is, of course, not mandatory language. Presumably, however, the findings of the International Authority would in practice have had a strongly persuasive effect.

direction on the controlling sector. ") The increase, however,
was to be subject to review by the international authority which
could "recommend an adjustment. "

Only once was the international authority to have power to
"request" rather than merely "recommend. " If, at least
three years after an increase under the escalator provision,
the airline's load factor on its busiest segment of the route
had averaged less than 50 percent over the preceding twelve
months, the international authority could "request the state
to reduce or withdraw the whole or part of the increased capacity. "

By contrast, the United Kingdom, in its Document 384,
proposed that Fifth Freedom traffic could not be used to justify
capacity at all. It could be carried, but only on a "fill-up"
basis. This meant simply that the capacity offered all along
the route would have to be based on Third Freedom, but that
aircraft scheduled in accordance with such capacity limitations
would be free to pick up Fifth Freedom passengers to fill any
empty seats. And there would often be empty seats since the
presumed load factor on which capacity would be based (60 or
65 percent) means that on an average flight 35 or 40 percent
of the seats are empty. Passenger loads naturally also vary
by days of the week and seasons.

The British were saying, in effect, that a United States
airline would have to shrink its capacity down from point to
point along the route in accordance with the Third Freedom
passengers left aboard the aircraft; having effected this
shrinkage, however, which would be quite severe for points
beyond Europe, the airline would have the compensation of
being allowed to fill empty space with Fifth Freedom.

But the British would then have put a further limitation
on even this fill-up traffic. It would have to be charged a
higher fare then if it traveled over a local airline, the fare
differential to be fixed by the international authority. A
London-Paris passenger, that is, would travel at a lower fare
on a British or French airline than if he picked up the flight
of an American airline which had come in from New York.

In terms of service to the Near and Middle East, the
United Kingdom proposal would have severely restricted United
States airline operations and might well have made round-the-
world service impossible even today, let alone in the era of
the Chicago Conference.

The Canadian Document sought a mid-point between the
United States and United Kingdom positions. In fact, it did
what an arbitrator will sometimes do--i.e., it "split the

difference. " By this is meant that, instead of merely permitting Fifth Freedom on a fill-up basis (per the United Kingdom), it would have allowed such traffic to be used as part of
the base for calculating the initial capacity, subject to the
arbitrary formula that for this initial calculation it would be
assumed that Fifth Freedom would equal one half the Third
Freedom.   The method of shrinking capacity by a system of
"sectors" and "divisions" was proposed, as in the United
States plan.   The United States, however, had thought of this
system as providing capacity based on Third Freedom without
review power in the international authority; Canada would see
it provide capacity based on Third Freedom with the arbitrary
allowance for presumed Fifth Freedom.   The assignment of
initial capacity would have to be by the international authority
(unpalatable to the United States), but the requesting state
would be "entitled" to a capacity based on the formula (highly
palatable to the United States).

The broad and vague provision in the American proposal
that an assumed Fifth Freedom allowance could be used in the
initial calculation, subject to review and "recommendation"
by the international authority, was omitted.   A minor liberaliza-
tion was that the load factor to be assumed in all calculations
was reduced to 60 percent from 65 percent.

The important escalator provision closely resembled that
of the United States, with the significant exception that it would
limit a capacity increase to a division (not to an entire route)
when the load factor over any sector in that division averaged
over 60 percent in either direction.   While this was substantially less liberal than the American plan, it should be remembered that this escalator would have been premised on an
initial capacity containing an allowance for Fifth Freedom as
described above.

At this point the three proposals may seem overly complex.
Indeed, Churchill later made reference to "the projects which
have succeeded one another in such profusion during the intricate discussions at Chicago. "[29] It should be kept in mind,
however, that had one of these proposals been adopted, its
formulas and calculations would have been worked, in future
years, by specialists in such matters within the international
authority, the governments, and the airlines.   Neither the
political officials of a government, nor its diplomats, much
less the traveling public, would have had to master the com-
plexities.

The Roosevelt-Churchill Correspondence

The clash betwen the United States and United Kingdom
positions resulted in reference to the Chief Executives of both
countries, whose personal messages began on November 21,
1944. They reflect four phases: (1) a deadlock as of that date,
(2) the introduction of the Canadian proposal (above described)
on November 27, (3) an informal understanding between the
two leaders that they would instruct their delegations to try
to reach agreement along lines proposed by Canada, and (4)
a failure to reach such an agreement, which was manifested
by a joint United States-United Kingdom motion at Chicago to
put the whole question off for later consideration by the
Interim Council of the Provisional International Civil Aviation
Organization (PICAO) which the Conference was in the process
of establishing. This motion was made on November 30.

The messages between the two wartime leaders are extremely interesting, and reflect their respective personalities
and literary styles. For purposes of this study, however,
only pertinent highlights will be quoted. [30]

President Roosevelt initiated the exchange with a telegram
dated November 21, beginning:

> The aviation conference is at an impasse be-
> cause of a square issue between our people and
> yours. We have met you on a number of points,
> notably an arrangement for regulation of rates and
> an arrangement by which the number of planes in
> the air shall be adjusted to the amount of traffic.
> This is as far as I can go. In addition, your
> people are now asking a limitation on the number
> of planes between points regardless of the traffic
> offering.

Roosevelt then argued that such a limitation would "place a
dead hand on the use of the great air trade routes." He urged
Churchill to "get into this yourself and give instructions,
preferably by telephone, to your people in Chicago so that we
can arrange, if possible, to agree."

This message correctly states that the United States was
prepared to have the number of planes in the air adjusted to
the amount of traffic. But it does not really focus on the fact
that an American airline, beginning at the end of the war with
highly trained crews and excellent aircraft, might attract so
many passengers between two foreign points as to justify an

"adjustment" based on such Fifth Freedom, resulting in no decrease, and perhaps even an increase, in capacity as its route progressed around the world.

The British Prime Minister's response the following day, approved by his Cabinet, summarized the United Kingdom position, indicated that "we cannot see our way to accept" the United States position, and proposed that the Conference finalize the many matters, such as the technical agreements, where there was little or no conflict, and then adjourn for a period of time during which the problem might be studied further by the two governments.

Roosevelt, in reply, took the position that the United Kingdom proposal would have the practical effect of making routes to distant points impossible, including the economic operation by a British carrier, for example, from London through to India. He also charged that small states with small reservoirs of home traffic, such as the Netherlands, might have difficulty under the British plan in launching any substantial service. He then added:

> We know perfectly well that we ought not to set up a situation in which our operators could wreck the local establishments between nearby countries, or so fill the air on long routes that nobody else could get in and survive. We are quite prepared to discuss limitations of pick-up traffic to assure that this does not happen. What we do want is sufficient play so that the establishment and maintenance of the long routes on a reasonably economic basis is possible. For your information, the Canadians are tackling the situation on that basis.

In another exchange, the President reiterated the United States position and went so far as to mention that it might be difficult to obtain generous lend-lease appropriations from Congress "if it and the people feel that the United Kingdom has not agreed to a generally beneficial air agreement."

In a lengthy reply, Churchill concluded that the whole matter required "further patient study." He again proposed an adjournment of "a few weeks or even months, while both parties persevered behind the scenes for a settlement." He needed, he said, to "make sure that Great Britain and the Dominions and many other countries as well were not in fact run out of the air altogether as a result of your flying start." And he indicated that he could not obtain the agreement of his Cabinet or Parliament to anything which "wore that aspect."

The attention then turned to the Canadian proposal,
Roosevelt stating on November 30 that:

> The Canadians undoubtedly see both points of
> view, have laboured tirelessly to bring us together
> and on November 27 brought out a new formula
> which might provide a reasonable line of com-
> promise if the small nations would indeed accept
> so limited a formula. I will give Berle latitude
> for one more try on the lines of that formula if
> you will give Swinton the same.

The crucial day was November 30. John Winant, the
United States Ambassador at London, followed up the President's message by urging on Churchill "the acceptance of the
Canadian compromise." With the United States thus apparently
ready to accept the Canadian plan, the two governments came
right to the edge of agreeing. The British Cabinet, Winant
was informed later that day, intended "to accept the compromise
but at the same time ask for a small passenger rate differential
on pickups on long hauls." (This was the Fifth Freedom fare
differential already proposed by the United Kingdom in Document 384.) However, before the decision could be forwarded
to the British Delegation at Chicago, "the Conference had ad-
journed."[31] (Actually, what had happened was not the adjournment of the Conference but the decision, announced publicly
by the United States and the United Kingdom jointly, to put the
question off to the Interim Council.)
　Winant's account is confirmed generally by a message
to the President from Churchill on December 1, although it
is not entirely clear that specific instructions were issued to
the delegation at Chicago. Instead, it is possible to interpret
Churchill's remarks as indicating merely that the Canadian
plan, plus a Fifth Freedom fare differential, was being tenta-
tively discussed between London and the British Delegation at
Chicago without a final decision.
　It is also possible to interpret the circumstances as reflecting an unwillingness to resolve the disagreement even
along such lines, and to perceive a possible United Kingdom
tactic to delay agreement in order to obtain the action really
desired--i.e., the temporary adjournment of the Conference
and reference of the problem to the interim council.
　The problem was, indeed, referred to the interim council,
but as will be seen it was never entirely resolved either by
that Council, by later ICAO Councils, or in any other manner,
and remains partly unresolved today.

Analysis of the Near Agreement

In attempting to sort out the merits of the conflict just
described, one is struck immediately by the curious incon-
sistency that Roosevelt and Berle should have leaned toward
an economic ideology of virtually opening the world's skies to
unregulated competition, while at home they epitomized the
New Deal economic philosophy where the necessity for regulating the domestic economy was not only recognized but
vigorously pursued.

The theory that the unregulated economy results in the
most efficient utilization of resources had, it would seem,
been about laid to rest by the experience of the Great Depression. Furthermore, the advocacy of virtually unregulated
world air routes was plainly inconsistent with the Roosevelt
Administration's earlier espousal of the Civil Aeronautics
Act of 1938 wherein United States airlines had been made into
a regulated public utility, partly for the express purpose of
promoting better air service.

The present writer considers it unfortunate that the
Canadian compromise was not adopted at Chicago. It is true
that there is no precise logic to premising capacity, in part,
on an arbitrary allowance for Fifth Freedom of 50 percent of
Third Freedom. But with any decision where some kind of
"drag," so to speak, must be placed on the operation of
economic forces, there is bound to be difficulty in arriving
at a logically precise basis for the degree of "drag."

Canada suggested that its admittedly elaborate scheme
for determining capacity should be placed in an annex to the
Convention, rather than in the Convention itself. In this way,
amendments could be made without the cumbersome process
of amending a treaty, with ratifications. A parallel procedure
was, in fact, established at Chicago with respect to air navigation and safety matters. Amendments to these "technical
annexes" are made by the ICAO Council from time to time; a
dissenting state may except itself from such an amendment,
but in doing so it would deny itself the advantages of uniform
world safety standards.

Given the uncertainty as to how the world's air services
were going to develop after the war, and the newness and indeed downright novelty of commercial airline service across
the oceans at that time, it seems understandable that the
British and other countries would fear that American airlines
might wholly dominate air travel. The Canadian proposal
would have limited the degree of such possible dominance, yet

at the same time allowed for development of substantial air
service by the American carriers beyond European gateways.
If in time, with the development of good service with good,
postwar aircraft by the other countries, the fear of United
States dominance had lessened, the annex could have been
amended accordingly.

THE OUTCOME AT CHICAGO

The outcome at Chicago was that neither the basic convention which established ICAO nor the Interim Agreement
which set up the Provisional Organization made any grant of
any of the Five Freedoms.* The Final Act contained a standard
form of bilateral agreement and advocated its use pending
the day when a multilateral agreement might be enacted. This
standard form, however, does not contain controversial points,
these being left for negotiation between the two parties in each
instance. Instead, it is concerned largely with "housekeeping"
details such as the right of an airline to bring in fuel and other
airline supplies duty free, and the right of the receiving state
to insist that an airline of another state be owned and controlled
by nationals of that state. [32]
Thus, it might appear that the Conference was, in effect,
telling the member states to go forth and negotiate bilateral
agreements, making all determinations as to routes, rates,
capacity, and Freedoms bilaterally. However, the Conference
also drew up and opened for signature two separate agreements,
with the understanding that some, but by no means all, of the
members would accept one or the other or both.

The "Two Freedoms" Agreement

The less controversial was the Transit or "Two Freedoms"
Agreement, which was expected to be accepted, and was accepted, by most of the ICAO member governments, and is in

---

*A minor exception is that the basic Convention (Article
5) grants the first two Freedoms to nonscheduled operations.
It also appears to grant traffic rights (i.e., the three other
Freedoms) to nonscheduled operations, but this is so hedged
with the right of states to impose conditions that, in practice,
it is virtually no grant at all. Proceedings, op. cit., p. 148.

effect today. As has been previously pointed out, it granted
the right to transit the territory of another state with scheduled
airlines and to make stops for fueling or other nontraffic
purposes. [33]

The controversial questions of Fifth Freedom, rates, and
capacity did not, of course, enter into this agreement; yet
they are indirectly involved because certain states geograph-
ically located athwart principal routes were conceding a substantial piece of their bargaining power with respect to future
bilateral agreements. This was of more significance in 1944
than today when long-range jet aircraft easily fly nonstop from
New York to Paris or from Tokyo to San Francisco. In those
days, the Azores, Newfoundland (which at that time was a
British colony rather than Canadian), and Hawaii, for example,
were highly important refueling points.

The "Five Freedoms" Agreement

The other agreement was known as the Transport or
"Five Freedoms" Agreement. Never widely adopted, it early
became virtually a dead letter. It was the creature of the
United States, and it seemed, at any rate, to be a device to
get as many countries as possible who agreed with the American
position at Chicago to join with the United States in a multilateral grant among themselves of the five Freedoms, without
the various capacity controls, the escalator, or rate controls
which had been proposed by other countries. [34]

The curious fact about this agreement is that it remains
unclear today whether the United States intended by it to surrender the right to require bilateral route agreements, or
whether, to the contrary, it intended that the freedoms
"granted" were to be exercised only along routes negotiated
bilaterally. There is even considerable evidence that certain
elements in the United States Government took the agreement
to mean the one thing and other elements took it to mean the
other.

If the agreement is to be interpreted as a sweeping multilateral grant of traffic rights, then various limitations in its
text become of heightened significance because they would
have served as the only checks on an otherwise wholly unregulated world airline regime.

Perhaps the most significant limitation was that a state
upon acceptance of the agreement, or at any later time on six
months' notice, might "elect not to grant and receive" the Fifth

Freedom rights. (Article IV, Section 1.) This, of course,
would be an action a state would not undertake lightly because,
by refusing Fifth Freedom to others it would lose the right for
its own airlines.

Another limitation was a rather generally worded provision
in Article III that:

> Each contracting State undertakes that in the
> establishment and operation of through services
> due consideration shall be given to the interests
> of other contracting States so as not to interfere
> unduly with their regional services or to hamper
> the development of their through services.

In the absence of any attempt to define when interference is
"undue, " or to set up an international body to make such determinations, this Article might have proved little more than a
point of departure for diplomatic discussions the outcome of
which would hinge on the general relationship of the two parties.
At best, the efficacy of the Article would have depended on
the good will of the disputing parties; at worst, it is no more
than a pious statement.

One limitation, however, had some "teeth" in it. If a
state felt that an action by another state "is causing injustice
or hardship to it, " it might appeal to the Council of ICAO.
(Article IV, Section 2.) The Council could recommend corrective action; if it subsequently found that a state should "unreasonably fail to take suitable corrective action, " it could
recommend to the ICAO Assembly that the state "be suspended
from its rights and privileges under this Agreement until such
action has been taken. " The Assembly could then have suspended the state by a two-thirds vote. The possible practical
defect existed that the penalty of suspension from all rights
under the Agreement might have seemed so drastic that the
Assembly might have been hesitant to take it, particularly
with a major power.

It seems scarcely likely that the United States, having
approached Chicago initially with proposals to leave economic
decisions outside the basic multilateral convention, would
come forth at the end of the Conference with a proposal granting routes and rights multilaterally in all directions to all
who would make the reciprocal grant. It seems a more likely
American view that bilateral route negotiations were to continue
to be necessary, and that the Five Freedoms Agreement simply
would have bound the signatories to operate the bilaterally-
negotiated routes in a certain fashion. This would have meant

that the United States, with its great bargaining power as the major traffic-generating nation in the world, could have done famously in route exchanges, and then enjoyed broad Fifth Freedom rights, with no capacity or rate controls.

Yet, to find specific support in the agreement for such an interpretation, it is necessary to put a rather improbable interpretation on a paragraph in Section 5 of Article I, which reads:

> Each contracting State may, subject to the provisions of this Agreement,
> (1) Designate the route to be followed within its territory by any international air service and the airports which any such service may use;

In aviation parlance, the word route is sometimes used (as usually in this study) to mean a series of cities to be served on a particular scheduled service. But the word can also be used to refer to the navigational path that an aircraft will follow. Every country designates the pathways through the air that airlines may travel; this is both a safety measure and a device to control foreign aircraft from a security standpoint. Certain airports are designated as ports of entry, where customs and immigration officials are stationed. The above-quoted language appears to be referring to a navigational path and to airports prepared to receive aircraft from a customs and immigration standpoint. Had it been intended to require separate bilateral route agreements, the reference would surely have been to "points" or "cities" rather than to "airports." Furthermore, the language appears identically in the Two Freedoms Agreement, where it could not possibly be referring to traffic rights. [35]

Berle at least appears to have looked upon the Agreement as obviating the need for bilateral agreements, as did another member of the Delegation, who is recognized as a leading scholar in international aviation, Dr. John C. Cooper. Neither man, however, is entirely unambiguous on this point. [36]

Later, after the United States had denounced this Agreement, one writer noted that it had "certain legal infirmities and obscurities which had not been foreseen." [37] Another writer has stated flatly that the agreement "provided that any signatory could initiate commercial service to and through the territory of any other signatory without further permission." [38]

Still later, a Netherlands aviation authority, looking back

on the era, stated that in the Five Freedoms Agreement, "more far-reaching obligations were laid down (control by States was almost entirely abolished). "[39]

Despite the views of these writers, it is interesting to note that the Civil Aeronautics Board of the United States, in a decision which by law had to be signed, and was signed, by the President, stated in 1946 that the Five Freedoms Agreement necessitated that there be route awards negotiated bilaterally on a basis of reciprocity. [40]

At any rate, the ambiguity of American intentions was clearly resolved in 1946, the year that notice of denunciation of the Five Freedoms Agreement was given. From that year onward, as will be seen, the United States has plainly insisted that any multilateral agreement bearing on Third, Fourth, and Fifth Freedoms should be operative only to the extent that each country obtains routes through bilateral negotiations. But prior to this clarification (and foreshadowing it) there came, a little over a year after the end of the Chicago Conference, the highly significant bilateral negotiation between the United States and the United Kingdom which took place at Bermuda and which has ever after made the word "Bermuda" a word of art in international aviation matters.

THE BERMUDA AGREEMENT

The Bermuda Agreement involved a reciprocal grant of airline routes, but its significance for this study is that it established a means for governing capacity and Fifth Freedom that differed appreciably from the various proposals that had been put forth at Chicago. These "Bermuda principles" are still in existence today as the governing ones between the two countries and between many other countries governed by other bilateral agreements modeled on this one.

The distinguishing characteristic of the Bermuda system of regulation is that in place of any formula or other method for predetermining capacity, or for justifying the carriage of certain amounts of Fifth Freedom, it substitutes a sweeping right of each airline to institute capacity in its own discretion and to carry Fifth Freedom traffic in its own discretion, subject only to ex post facto action if a government complains that the capacity being offered or the Fifth Freedom traffic actually being carried violates certain general principles.

The basic principle is set forth in a lengthy paragraph

(Paragraph 6) in the agreement which states, in part, that the services provided by an airline "shall retain as their primary objective the provision of capacity adequate to the traffic demands between the country of which such air carrier is a national and the country of ultimate destination of the traffic."[41] (See Appendix A for the full text of Paragraph 6.)

This can be taken to mean that the amount of Fifth Freedom traffic being carried over any part of a route must not exceed the amount of Third/Fourth Freedom. It would be reasonable to say that an airline carrying more Fifth than Third/Fourth no longer has Third/Fourth as its "primary objective." However, it is also possible to read the sentence as permitting, for example, a daily flight between the home country and the other country, justified as the service necessary to be "adequate to the traffic demands" between the two points, even though the Fifth Freedom may exceed the Third/ Fourth. The contention can be advanced that, where countries of substantial size and with significant cultural or economic ties are involved, the public expects, and is entitled to, a daily service, even though such a service cannot be operated economically without having Fifth Freedom exceed Third/Fourth.

The foregoing is not the only ambiguous sentence in the Bermuda Agreement by any means. Indeed, the remaining language of Paragraph 6 appears to lend itself to repeated difficult ex post facto consultations. There are no formulas whatever, no mathematical quantities whatsoever, to be employed as benchmarks. This language--which despite its vagueness is really the heart of the Bermuda principles--states that the right to carry Fifth Freedom traffic:

> . . . shall be applied in accordance with the general principles of orderly development to which both Governments subscribe and shall be subject to the general principle that capacity should be related: (a) to traffic requirements between the country of origin and the countries of destination; (b) to the requirements of through airline operation; and (c) to the traffic requirements of the area through which the airline passes after taking account of local and regional services.

The present writer would interpret the Bermuda concept as a sort of "gentlemen's agreement" not to do anything that is too unreasonable, or at least not to expect to go on doing it for any great length of time. Thus, an airline may establish

what capacity it pleases and proceed to accept Fifth Freedom
to the extent it wishes in the knowledge, however, that if over
a period of time it operates at consistently low load factors
or if it is filling its seats with predominantly Fifth Freedom
traffic, it may well be called upon to justify its service in
terms of Paragraph 6.

In a consultation, the airline (or actually its government
on its behalf) may select, for example, the "requirements of
through airline operation" language and contend that it cannot
fly from New York to India on any economic basis without
taking a predominance of Fifth Freedom traffic over the
farthest sectors. The argument can also be made that the airline conducting this through service, while it carries some
local and regional traffic into and out of India from and to
countries adjacent to India, nevertheless offers, say, only
one daily flight whereas the "local and regional services" offer
far more numerous flights. Therefore, the latter services
have been "taken into account," per the language of Paragraph
6, in the sense that they are not being seriously injured by
the through airline.

The other government, however, may choose to emphasize
the language referring to "traffic requirements between the
country of origin and the countries of destination," make a
strict count of Third/Fourth Freedom traffic, and then contend
that under the "primary objective" language the amount of
capacity being offered is not justified.

The agreement includes an elaborate rate-regulating device whereby primary reliance is placed on the carrier organization, the International Air Transport Association.* In practice,
the IATA carriers establish the basic structure of rates which

---

*The International Air Transport Association (IATA) was
founded in 1945 as successor to an earlier European association of airlines. Membership is open to any scheduled airline
whose government belongs (or is eligible to belong) to ICAO.
Its headquarters activities are divided between Montreal and
Geneva, with a permanent staff under a Director General subject to control of an annual General Meeting of the member
airlines. Its most important function is the making of rate
agreements (subject to government approvals) for which it
convenes Traffic Conferences for different areas of the world.
(This function is the one of particular interest to the present
study.) Another function is to serve as a clearing house
through which airline accounts for interline revenues are
settled. IATA may be contrasted with the International Civil

the several airlines then charge, and while IATA actions are
subject to the approval of each government, such approval is
usually given. Where it is denied, further consultations
among the carriers through the conference machinery (and
sometimes among their governments) follow until agreement
is reached.

While the Bermuda Agreement emphasizes ex post facto
consultations between the two governments, it also permits
reference of a dispute which cannot be settled by consultation
to the ICAO Council for an advisory opinion. This procedure,
however, has never been used.

It was anticipated by some that if a sufficient number of
countries used the Bermuda principles in their bilateral agreements, a system would grow wherein there would be so much
uniformity that the drafting of a multilateral agreement would
be facilitated. The main question here, as will shortly be
seen, was whether such a multilateral agreement was to involve a basic multilateral grant of traffic rights or whether it
was merely to universalize the principles of capacity, Fifth
Freedom, and rate control, leaving the route grants for continued bilateral negotiations.

The Bermuda Agreement was signed in February, 1946.
Then, on September 19, 1946, a joint statement was issued
by the United States and the United Kingdom indicating that
both governments would endeavor to include all the Bermuda
principles in their future bilateral agreements with other
countries, and that they considered that these principles might
form a basis for a future multilateral agreement.

The Bermuda language, while still tending to be the governing concept in international air transport today, has been

---

Aviation Organization (ICAO) which is a governmental body
established by treaty drawn up at the Chicago Conference, is
a specialized agency of the United Nations, and has the general
structure found in such agencies--i. e. , a permanent international civil service under a Secretary General at its headquarters in Montreal, a Council consisting of representatives
of certain of the governments which functions as a Board of
Directors, and an Assembly of all the member governments
which meets periodically to exercise general control over both
Council and Secretariat. Certain of the functions of ICAO
overlap functions of IATA, notably the making of legal, economic, and safety studies. However, ICAO is the effective
organization for establishing safety and navigation standards,
while IATA is the effective organization in rate making.

variously modified in different bilateral agreements so that
some actually have what is virtually a negation of one of the
Bermuda precepts--a predetermination of capacity. The expression "heavy Bermuda" is used for these more restrictive
agreements, as against a "light Bermuda" agreement. [42]

THE 1946 DRAFT
OF A MULTILATERAL AGREEMENT

It will be recalled that a Provisional Civil Aviation Organization (PICAO) had been provided for by the Chicago Conference to serve as an interim body pending ratification of the
basic Convention by twenty-six governments, the number required to put the latter Convention into effect and permit activa-
tion of the permanent International Civil Aviation Organization
(ICAO). The provisional body began operations in August,
1945, at Montreal, and functioned until April, 1947, when the
permanent body took over.

One of the first tasks of the Provisional International
Civil Aviation Organization when it began operations in August,
1945, was to draft a multilateral convention on the matters
that had caused the great disagreement at Chicago.

The PICAO Council assigned the task to a newly established
Air Transport Committee, to be assisted by an arm of the
PICAO Secretariat called the Air Transport Bureau. The Air
Transport Committee was open to representatives of all member governments, a sort of "committee of the whole." (When
the permanent organization, ICAO, came into being in 1947,
it limited the membership to twelve.) The "1946 Draft," as
it came to be called, was prepared by this Committee and
was submitted to the PICAO plenary body, the Assembly, in
the spring of 1946. [43]

Analysis of the Draft

The Draft took elements from various of the Chicago and
Bermuda concepts. [44] It took from the Five Freedoms Agreement the concept of a general grant of the Five Freedoms
without necessity for bilateral negotiation of routes (assuming
that the ambiguous Five Freedoms document is to be interpreted in this manner). However, unlike the Five Freedoms
Agreement, which placed no limitation on capacity, on

proportion of Fifth Freedom, or on rates (other than some
very general language), and equally unlike the various Chicago
drafts of capacity formulas and escalator clauses, this Draft
used the Bermuda capacity language. In addition, though, it
established the concept of a rate differential on Fifth Freedom
traffic, a point which had been suggested by the British and
Canadians at Chicago as a device to break the deadlock. The
Draft "suggests" a 10 percent maximum differential. *

The most remarkable feature was that, far from leaving
the settlement of disputes to bilateral consultations, as in the
Bermuda system, with use of the Council of ICAO purely for
advisory opinions, the Draft would have established an "International Civil Air Transport Board" with extensive powers,
much along the lines recommended by Canada in its original
proposal at Chicago. The bilateral consultation would be encouraged as an initial step, but where it failed, an aggrieved
party could place the dispute before the Board. The latter
had extensive powers to investigate grievances, conduct hearings, and "order the corrective action necessary." (Article
29.)

The board would have consisted of from five to seven
members, to be elected by the Assembly. Its competence
would have been limited to grievances of the following four
types:

1. Unreasonably high or low rates.
2. Unfair competitive practices or unfair subsidies.
3. Inadequacy of a Fifth Freedom rate differential, or
hardship resulting from one.
4. The "operation or threatened operation of excessive
capacity by airlines." Ordinarily there would be no predetermination of capacity, and the airlines would have "reasonable
discretion"--in the language of Article 15--to decide what
capacity to employ. Article 15 goes on to say, however, that
each State must keep its airlines from "unduly continuing to
operate excessive capacity" or even "initiating capacity obviously in excess of requirements and intended for destructively
competitive services."

The comment was made earlier that the Bermuda system
was, in a sense, a gentlemen's agreement not to do anything
too unreasonable. There seems a similar element present in

---

*A summary of pertinent portions of the 1946 Draft ap-
pears as Appendix B.

these capacity provisions, with the important difference that when something too unreasonable is happening there can be an appeal to an International Board with authority to do something about it.

Only a state could be a party to a board proceeding--i.e., an airline would have to be represented by its government. Any board decision could be appealed within thirty days to the Council which could affirm or void the decision, or refer it back to the board for further proceedings. If the board's decision was not appealed, or was appealed but upheld by the Council, the language of the Draft (Article 33) states that all parties "shall conform" to the decision and shall require their airlines to conform. Otherwise, the board "shall certify the failure to the Council," which might, in its discretion--

1. "Authorize or require" any state to prohibit the operation in its airspace of an airline or all airlines of a state which is not conforming.

2. Recommend to the Assembly that the state "be suspended from any or all of its rights and privileges under this agreement." (The Assembly could take such action by a two-thirds vote.)

Procedurally, the board was to have been modeled on regulatory bodies such as those of the United States Government--e.g., the Interstate Commerce Commission and the Civil Aeronautics Board. It could direct that hearings be conducted by a hearing examiner or by one board member, after which the whole board would hear argument at the request of any party and would then issue a decision. In a provision resembling the power of subpoena of regulatory bodies in the United States, Article 36 provides that each state "agrees to make available to the board and its representatives any information (other than information classified as secret and confidential for reasons of national defense) reasonably required for the proper discharge of the board's duties, and to require its nationals to do likewise upon the request of the board."

With respect to rates, the 1946 Draft apparently sought, as it did with the capacity problem, to leave the matter ordinarily in the hands of the individual airlines or governments, but to provide effective, mandatory board action (subject to appeal to the Council) where consultations among the governments did not produce agreement.

Thus, the Draft stated that either the airlines or an airline

conference, or a government or governments, might initiate
rates or rate changes. A state objecting to a rate would first
consult the other affected states. In the absence of agreement,
any state could take the matter to the board. The Draft would
have given the board guidance in determining what constitutes
a reasonable rate, by language in Article 20 reading: "Rates
shall be deemed unreasonable if they are found by the board
to depart unduly from the level indicated by the costs of the
most economic comparable operator, plus a profit reasonable
in the circumstances. "

Although this language may seem rather general, it is
more specific than that found in the regulatory statutes for
transportation media in the United States. The Federal Aviation Act of 1958, for example, gives to the Civil Aeronautics
Board merely the guidance that domestic rates shall be "just
and reasonable" and that neither domestic nor international
rates may show "any unjust discrimination or any undue or
unreasonable prejudice or disadvantage" to any person, type
of traffic, or locality. [45] The International Civil Air Transport
Board envisaged by the 1946 Draft would have had the right to
look deeply into the economics of the several competing airlines over a route where a rate had been questioned. It would
have made a determination as to the costs of the lowest-cost
competitor and would even have decided what was a reasonable
margin of profit for that operator. It would then have used
the result as an index for the rate to be charged.

This, in practice, would have permitted the most efficient
operator to reduce fares down to a point indicated by its costs
plus a small profit. This might well give such an airline a
substantial competitive weapon against its competitors since
they (in light of the undifferentiated nature of the product)
would have to reduce their fares to the same level even though
the result for them would be a loss operation chargeable against
profits from elsewhere in their systems or against subsidy
paid by their governments. The consumer would benefit, however, in that he would not be subsidizing the less efficient
operators. There could even be hope that the latter would
feel pressured to seek diligently to improve their operations.

It would, of course, have been a difficult problem for the
board to have applied in specific cases such portions of the
above-quoted language as that which states that a rate is unreasonable if found "to depart unduly from the level indicated
by the costs of the most economic comparable operator. "
The board would find that the determination of what it costs
to conduct airline service over a particular route is an

elaborate science far more difficult than may at first be supposed, and made even more difficult where an airline wishes
its records to lead to a particular conclusion.   Yet this is
something that is done every day by the United States Government regulatory agencies, even though there are large areas
of judgment involved.   The proposed board could, in a manner
parallel to that of the United States agencies, have required
cost and revenue data from the airlines, then used the hearing procedure to arrive at a determination of the level at
which the most economic operator could conduct his service.

    Another problem would have been to define "to depart un-
duly. " Conceivably a low-cost operator could experiment
with a fare which appeared to "depart unduly" from an economic level, but which would be defended by the proposing
airline as likely to promote enough new traffic to support itself.   Presumably the board would allow such a fare for a
period of time and then determine whether it appeared to be
unreasonable.   The judgment factor, however, is once again
clear; the system depended on a grant of fairly broad discretion to an international agency.

    The rate-making provisions of the 1946 Draft seem to be
sensible ones.   They would have left the elaborate intricacies
of international rates to the airlines or airline conferences so
far as possible, and to intergovernmental consultations to the
extent that governments felt it necessary to intervene.   They
would have involved the international machinery only on appeal by an aggrieved party.   However, once invoked, the international machinery would have had compulsory powers,
subject to appeal to the ICAO Council, applying ratemaking
guidelines which, in the opinion of the present writer, are as
specific as circumstances will allow and well oriented toward
the interest of the consumer.

    By contrast, the only international machinery provided
by the Bermuda Agreement was an advisory opinion of the
ICAO Council.   But a dispute over rates is characteristically
even more intricate than a dispute over capacity or Fifth
Freedom, and calls for extensive expertise in cost analysis.
If an advisory opinion on a rate were ever requested of the
Council, it would scarcely be competent or willing to devote
the time and attention necessary to resolving the dispute.
More than likely it would set up some sort of ad hoc body to
report to it, but such a body, not possessing a permanent
staff of experts nor subpoena powers, could scarcely do an
adequate job.

    In short, if there is to be any effective international body

in matters of rates, it appears necessary that it be an expert
regulatory body along lines of the United States regulatory
agencies, as the 1946 Draft sought to establish.

To implement the type of regulation envisaged by the
Draft, each government would have to accept, by treaty, the
obligation to enforce rulings of the international body, much
as governments today enforce within their jurisdictions the
navigation and safety standards of ICAO. The administrative
problems of a worldwide regulatory body would be particularly
difficult with respect to rates because of the large number of
cities and areas, the differing characteristics of the markets,
and the necessity for dealing with so many airlines and governments.

However, this elaborate regulation of rates is undertaken
today, in a sense, by the International Air Transport Association (IATA), while the Civil Aeronautics Board regulates, with
a very small staff, an American domestic jurisdiction which
includes services as distant and different as local-service
carriers serving minor cities and long-range carriers flying
to such points as Puerto Rico, Alaska, and Hawaii. In any
event, the 1946 Draft would have left most day-to-day problems
with the airlines, IATA, and the governments, with the international regulatory body handling only those cases that were
appealed to it. To resolve the latter, however, would indeed
pose difficult judgments requiring development of standards
and expertise. The methods and administrative problems in
connection with the 1946 Draft, or a possible similar regime,
will be discussed in further detail in the concluding chapter
of this study.

PICAO Rejects the 1946 Draft

The PICAO Assembly, meeting in the late spring of 1946,
could come to no position favorable to the Draft, nor did it
succeed in coming to any other conclusion as to what should
go in a multilateral agreement. It nevertheless passed a
resolution that "a multilateral agreement on commercial
rights in international civil air transport constitutes the only
solution compatible with the character of the International
Civil Aviation Organization. "[46]

Comments by various governments on the Draft were subsequently published by the PICAO Secretariat. [47] In general,
they were unfavorable, particularly on the basic point of establishing an International Civil Air Transport Board. Of the

larger aviation powers, only Australia, Canada, and India
seemed to favor the proposal, but Australia hedged by saying
that it should be "subject to more careful examination" and
Canada hedged to the extent of saying that it would be willing
to consider any alternatives anyone wished to propose.

The United Kingdom submitted a proposal departing considerably from its approach at Chicago and adopting the basic
Bermuda concept of bilaterally negotiated routes with "Bermuda
principles," without any International Board, and with only
advisory powers in PICAO in case of disputes.

The United States took a strongly negative view, concentrating its force on the concept of a board with compulsory
powers. It contended that the world lacked expertise in international air transportation problems, which lack would make
it difficult for such a board or any international organization
to assume the responsibility for making final, binding decisions,
especially "in view of the generality of the language it would
be called upon to construe." It was argued that the advisory
opinion procedure whereby the Council of ICAO would issue
opinions "relying for their effectiveness upon their moral
force and the public opinion created by their publication,"
would permit the development of experience so that in the
future it could be determined "whether increased responsibility should be imposed."[48]

THE 1947 DRAFT OF A
MULTILATERAL AGREEMENT

In the fall and winter of 1946-7, the Air Transport Committee of PICAO, working through a subcommittee, prepared
a further Draft which was circulated in March, 1947.[49]

As in the case of the 1946 Draft, this document rejected
bilateral route bargaining and established principles to govern
capacity, Fifth Freedom, and rates along lines of Bermuda
but even more general in language.* It differed from the 1946
Draft chiefly in that it would have established no international
board. Instead, as with the Bermuda Agreement itself, it
provided for settlement of disputes by bilateral consultations
and by reference, where necessary, to the ICAO Council, but
with the difference that the Council was to be empowered to do

---

*Pertinent provisions of the 1947 Draft appear as Ap-
pendix C.

far more than issue an advisory opinion; it instead could issue
a temporary restraining order if necessary, and could establish an arbitral tribunal whose decisions would be binding on
the states and airlines concerned in the dispute. [50]

Perhaps the most significant thing about the 1947 Draft,
however, is that it was accompanied by a dissenting report
which, while representing the views of a minority, included
the two major aviation powers, the United States and the
United Kingdom, as well as China. The minority view was
set forth as an appendix to the committee report. It proposed
that the multilateral agreement state unequivocally that grant
of traffic rights is a matter for bilateral negotiation.* The
only amelioration of this strict bilateral position was a provision that--

> No Contracting State shall decline an exchange
> of routes with any other Contracting State on any
> grounds other then an insufficiency of traffic to
> justify the proposed operations, or otherwise dis-
> criminate unfairly against any such State. [51]

Such a provision would have been an advance over the
present system whereby a route may be denied on any grounds
or for unstated reasons. Nevertheless, the expression "insufficiency of traffic," whether referring to traffic currently
moving over the route or to traffic that could be expected to
move if an additional airline offered service, is an expression
with so great a judgment factor in it that it might not have
served to limit bilateral negotiations to questions of airline
economics. Thus, a country desiring to deny a route from
some political motive might allege that current and prospective
traffic was "insufficient" to justify an additional airline. Yet
the minority report accepted the provision of binding arbitration which the majority had proposed; in light of this interesting
and perhaps significant concession by the United States and
the United Kingdom, the refusal of a government to grant a
route via bilateral negotiation could presumably have become
the subject of binding arbitration interpreting the above-quoted
language.

The minority contended that a multilateral exchange of
rights would lead to "friction and disputation." It appeared to
base its opposition largely on the relatively undeveloped nature

---

*Pertinent provisions of the minority report may be found
in Appendix D.

of international civil aviation, and particularly on the situation then existing where many states wishing to establish substantial airline services would be unable to do so pending postwar reconstruction. The minority contended that under these circumstances the majority's proposal would "permit the uneconomic duplication of existing services between pairs of States having substantial amounts of air traffic between themselves," and "tend to deprive States at present unable to take their proper part in international civil aviation of the possibility of safeguarding their future interests."[52]

It should be noted that there was no mention made in the minority report of the obvious strong economic and political interest of both the United Kingdom and the United States in retaining the right to grant or withhold routes to other governments. As the possessors of large and scattered land areas and having substantial populations with high income levels, each country doubtless realized that it held extremely great bargaining counters in any bilateral negotiation. To the present writer it appears particularly regrettable that the minority report could not have spoken to this point with some candor instead of omitting it altogether.

As to the concern of the minority with safeguarding the interests of states unable at the time to institute air service, it should be noted that the majority included several states with great future interest in international airlines that had only recently been released from German occupation: Czechoslovakia, France, Norway, Holland.

Almost as if in rebuttal of the minority report, the majority defended its route multilateralism by stating:

> A so-called multilateral agreement which left room for substantial items such as routes to be settled by bilateral negotiations would in fact be nothing more than a revised form of standard bilateral agreement . . . . If nations, each sovereign of its own territory, are left to bargain for the exchange of rights in international civil air transport in limited and varying degrees, the bargainings will be sources of conflict. Such bargainings will be in their nature discriminatory, and will involve even the possibility of an injection into the negotiations of points alien to aviation.[53]

The 1947 Draft and the minority report were submitted
through the Council to the Assembly of ICAO.* The Assembly
decided that in light of the minority position there was insufficient agreement among the governments to warrant the approval of either the 1947 Draft or the minority's alternative.
Instead, the Assembly decided to call a conference to continue
the work of attempting to arrive at a multilateral agreement.[54]

THE GENEVA CONFERENCE OF 1947

The Geneva Conference took place in November, 1947,
lasted for three weeks, and resulted in failure to conclude an
agreement. It was considered to be the first session of an
ICAO "Commission on Multilateral Agreement on Commercial
Rights in International Civil Air Transport," yet it amounted,
in effect, to a plenary meeting of governments. Thirty states
sent delegations, while three others sent observers, as did
the United Nations, the International Air Transport Association, and the International Chamber of Commerce.
Although the meeting was supposed to build its work on
the 1947 Draft which (in the majority version) had favored an
end to bilateral route negotiation, it arrived at the opposite
conclusion when it was less than halfway through its session.
In its seventh meeting, on the ninth day of the conference, it
adopted by a substantial majority the following motion:

> MOVED, That the Commission decides that its
> further discussions shall be based on the hypotheses:
> (1) that the granting of routes is to be accomplished
> through route agreements among the particular
> parties concerned; and
> (2) that the Multilateral Agreement will impose no
> obligation on its parties to enter into route agree-
> ments, entry into any such route agreements re-
> maining entirely discretionary with the parties con-
> cerned.[55]

---

*Shortly after publication of the 1947 Draft, the permanent
organization, ICAO, came into existence with the deposit of
the requisite number of ratifications of the appropriate Chicago
Convention. Thus, although drawn up by a committee of the
provisional organization, the Draft was submitted to the First
Assembly of the permanent organization, which met in May,
1947.

Only the Netherlands voted against this resolution, although six countries, all significant in international aviation,
abstained. Those were Australia, Canada, Colombia, Denmark, Ireland, and Norway.

In a sense, the effort to obtain a multilateral agreement
was defeated at that point. The Conference, however, went
on from there seeking to obtain an agreement which would
declare various principles to govern airline operations over
routes obtained by bilateral bargaining. This was, of course,
what the United States and the United Kingdom wanted.

It appeared for a time thereafter that the Conference was
going to conclude an agreement along the lines of the minority
report of the 1947 Draft--i.e., the Bermuda principles as to
capacity and Fifth Freedom. Thus, a draft was prepared de-
lineating a right to carry Fifth Freedom traffic to an extent
"related to the traffic requirements of the areas through which
the airline operates, after taking account of the special position
of local and regional air services."[56] Similarly, rate provisions were drafted which closely resembled those of Bermuda,
favoring setting of rates by airline conferences, subject to the
approval of governments, with disagreements being resolved
where possible by intergovernmental consultations.

Where such consultations (whether as to rates, Fifth
Freedom, or capacity) failed, there was to be a procedure
more complex than that in the Bermuda Agreement, which had
provided only for an advisory opinion by the ICAO Council.
(The proposals for third party settlement described herein
were prepared by a Drafting Committee at Geneva and "considered" but not actually voted on by the full Conference.)
There was to be reference to the International Court of Justice,
at the request of any party to a dispute, if it fell within the
subject matter set forth in Article 36(2) of the Statute of the
Court.* The decision of the Court would be binding.

However, an alternative mechanism, which involved use
of an arbitral tribunal, was not to be the right of any one
party to a dispute but, instead, required the prior consent of
all the parties to the dispute. A panel of persons competent
to serve on such arbitral tribunals was to have been established

---

*This subject matter, in the language of Article 36(2) of
the Statute, consists of: ". . . (a) the interpretation of a
treaty; (b) any question of international law; (c) the existence
of any fact which, if established, would constitute a breach of
an international obligation; (d) the nature or extent of the repara-
tion to be made for the breach of an international obligation."

by the President of the International Court of Justice after
consultation with the ICAO Council. [57]

One portion of the Bermuda concept, however, was not
acceptable to the majority of the delegates, and it was here
that the Conference finally came to a deadlock. This was the
concept that every bilateral agreement should grant Fifth
Freedom rights limited only by the general principle which
tended to put Fifth Freedom in a secondary position in justifying a particular capacity. After much discussion, a resolution
was proposed by Mexico which was carried by a vote of thirteen
to nine, with five abstentions and two delegates absent. This
resolution proposed a new article, to be added to the draft
agreement, which stated flatly that nothing in the agreement
would prevent a state from entering into a bilateral route
agreement limited to the carriage of Third and Fourth Freedom traffic. [58]

The implication of such an article is, of course, plain.
To use Mexico, the initiator of the resolution, as an example,
the effect would be to permit Mexico and the United States to
negotiate a bilateral agreement exchanging routes whereon the
United States airline, while permitted to fly to Mexico City
and beyond to other Latin American points, would be prohibited
from carrying traffic originating, for example, in Mexico City
and going on to such Latin American points. Generally speak-
ing, the vote appears to reflect a fear by those countries which
were not technologically advanced (or, in today's parlance,
underdeveloped countries) that their own air services could
not compete, either technologically or simply in the matter of
passenger preference, with those of the highly developed
nations.

Thus, of the five Latin American countries in attendance
at Geneva, four voted for the resolution and the other abstained. In addition, other underdeveloped countries voted
for the resolution, such as Egypt, Greece, India, Portugal,
and Turkey. In fact, the list of those supporting the resolution
is a list of underdeveloped nations plus the British Commonwealth countries, Australia, Canada, and New Zealand.

By contrast, the vote against the Mexican proposal and
in favor of the liberal grant of Fifth Freedom consisted of the
United States and the United Kingdom, plus seven Western
European nations.

Adoption of the Mexican resolution led to statements by
the United States and the United Kingdom that an agreement
containing such a provision would simply not be acceptable
to their governments. It was then decided that in light of the

basic divergence of views it would not be justifiable to submit to ICAO the text of any agreement in a form to be recommended for signature. Instead, the commission submitted the results of its work to the Assembly, including a tentative text* which it recommended be used as a premise for further deliber- tions.[59] The text includes the Mexican resolution.[60]

The Geneva Conference was the last major attempt to obtain a multilateral agreement on commercial rights. As will be seen, there were further discussions in the Council and Assembly of ICAO, but these were desultory and appear to have been engaged in without much hope of practical results. The era of an energetic struggle to get such an agreement may be said, therefore, to have begun at Chicago in 1944 and ended almost exactly three years later at Geneva.

Thus, since 1947, the economic regulation of the airlines of the world has consisted of the following: (1) The right of entry is governed by bilateral agreements; (2) the frequency and capacity of service are determined by the airline and (where domestic law requires) by its own government, but are subject to the ex post facto control of the Bermuda principles, except that in many bilateral agreements it is required that a frequency or capacity increase have the prior approval of the foreign government; (3) rate regulation rests initially with the airlines through the conferences of the International Air Transport Association (IAIA), subject to the approval of all rate changes by the various governments.

NOTES

1. John C. Cooper, The Right To Fly, (New York: Henry Holt & Co., 1947), pp. 143-5.

2. Jacob Schenkman, International Civil Aviation Organiza- tion, (Geneva: Librairie R. Droz, 1955), pp. 45-7.

3. Cooper, op. cit., p. 140.

4. Schenkman, op. cit., pp. 31-4; and R. R. Hackford, "Our International Aviation Policy," Harvard Business Re- view, 25:484, 1947.

---

*Pertinent provisions of this Geneva Draft appear as Appendix E.

5. United States Department of State, Proceedings of the International Civil Aviation Conference, Vol. I (Washington: Government Printing Office, 1948), pp. 55-62.

6. United States Department of State, Foreign Relations of the United States, 1944, Vol. II (Washington: Government Printing Office, 1967), pp. 360-2.

7. Ibid., pp. 423, 481, and 499.

8. Ibid., p. 451.

9. Ibid., pp. 563-4.

10. Ibid., pp. 450 and 563.

11. Ibid., p. 452.

12. Proceedings, op. cit., pp. 79-80.

13. Ibid., p. 83.

14. Foreign Relations, op. cit., pp. 503, 547-8.

15. Sigrid Arne, United Nations Primer, (New York: Farrar & Rinehart, Inc., 1945), pp. 89-90.

16. Dr. D. Goedhuis, Idea and Interest in International Aviation (The Hague: Martinus Nijhoff, 1947), p. 15.

17. Schenkman, op. cit., pp. 65-6; John C. Cooper, "International Ownership and Operation of World Air Transport Service" (Princeton University, 1946), pp. 128-42. (Mimeographed.)

18. The full Canadian proposal is set forth in Proceedings, op. cit., pp. 67-74.

19. Foreign Relations, op. cit., pp. 431-8 and 440.

20. Ibid., pp. 452-4.

21. The full text of the White Paper is in Proceedings, op. cit., pp. 566-70.

22. Foreign Relations, op. cit. , pp. 441-2. (Lord Beaver-brook was Lord Privy Seal in the British Cabinet at the time.)

23. Foreign Relations, op. cit. , p. 509.

24. Foreign Relations, op. cit. , pp. 516-19.

25. Ibid. , pp. 571-80.

26. Proceedings, op. cit. , pp. 595-604.

27. Ibid. , pp. 604-8.

28. Ibid. , pp. 610-14. Also, on page 615 appears a brief Canadian draft (Conference Document 410) which would merely have had the effect of transferring the substance of Article XI to an annex to the Convention.

29. Foreign Relations, op. cit. , p. 598.

30. The messages appear in Foreign Relations, op. cit. , pp. 584-99.

31. Foreign Relations, op. cit. , p. 596.

32. Proceedings, op. cit. , pp. 127-9.

33. The full text of the Agreement appears in Proceedings, op. cit. , pp. 175-8.

34. The full text of the Agreement appears in Proceedings, op. cit. , pp. 179-83.

35. Article I, Transit Agreement, Proceedings, op. cit. , pp. 175-6.

36. See Foreign Relations, op. cit. , pp. 607-9, and Cooper, The Right To Fly, op. cit. , pp. 179-81.

37. Virginia Little, "Control of International Air Transport, " International Organization, 3:34, February, 1949.

38. R. R. Hackford, "The International Aviation Policy of the United States" (unpublished Doctoral Dissertation, Harvard University, 1948), p. 331.

39. H. A. Wassenbergh, Post-War International Civil Aviation Policy and the Law of the Air (The Hague: Martinus Nijhoff, 1962), p. 17.

40. The Venezuela Case, Dockets 2180, 2281, and 2318, decided August 15, 1946. Civil Aeronautics Board Reports (Washington: Government Printing Office, 1948) 7:317-35.

41. The full text of the Agreement appears in Treaties and Other International Acts 1507 (Washington: Government Printing Office, 1946).

42. Wassenbergh, op. cit., p. 18.

43. Schenkman, op. cit., pp. 107, 114, 175-6, 311.

44. The full text of the Draft appears in PICAO Document 1577-AT/116 (Montreal: Provisional International Aviation Organization, 1946.)

45. 72 Stat. 788 (1958), U.S.C., 1301-1542, Section 404 (a) and (b).

46. PICAO Journal, 1:61, June, 1946.

47. PICAO Document 2089-EC/57.

48. PICAO Document 2089, op. cit., pp. 147-8.

49. Wassenbergh, op. cit., p. 18.

50. The complete text of the 1947 Draft Agreement appears in PICAO Document 4014, A-1-EC/1 as Appendix A.

51. Ibid., p. 39.

52. Ibid., p. 38.

53. Ibid., p. 11.

54. Schenkman, op. cit., pp. 318-9.

55. ICAO Document 5230, A2-EC/10, p. 173.

56. Ibid., p. 128.

57.   Articles 21-2 of the Draft Text prepared by a Drafting Committee at Geneva.   ICAO Document 5230, op. cit., pp. 144-5.

58.   ICAO Document 5230, op. cit., pp. 207-8.

59.   ICAO Document 5230, op. cit., pp. 129-30.

60.   The full text of the Draft Agreement appears on pp. 134-50 of Document 5230, op. cit.

3

The story of efforts to obtain a multilateral agreement in the 1948-69 era may be broken down into three parts: (1) 1948-53, (2) 1953-69 with respect to the Western European region, (3) 1953-69 with respect to a worldwide agreement.

Between 1948 and 1953 the member states of ICAO made further efforts through the ICAO mechanism, but met with no success, and there was no special conference or other major review of the subject in this time.

In 1953, the ICAO Assembly, seemingly despairing of success for a worldwide agreement, turned its attention to an initiative which had arisen in the Council of Europe and proposed that an effort be made to obtain a regional multilateral agreement limited to services within Western Europe. The second portion of this chapter will, therefore, deal with the European regional experience which, as will be seen, involved intense efforts but limited results.

The third portion of this chapter will be concerned with the attitudes, between the 1953 Assembly and 1969, of the various governments toward a worldwide multilateral agreement.

THE 1948-53 PERIOD

The Second Assembly

The Second Assembly of ICAO, meeting in 1948, concluded, after reviewing the work of the Geneva Conference,

66

that further efforts should be made to arrive at an agreement.
It asked the member states to submit further data, comments,
and suggestions to the ICAO Council which the latter would
review, then report upon to a future Assembly. [1]

The Fourth Assembly

So meager were the results of the above request that
two years later (1950) the Council, in submitting the replies
to the Fourth Assembly, recommended that the Assembly
should not even discuss the substantive issues since the replies "offered little hope that renewed discussions in the very
near future would have any useful results."[2]

Despite this negative recommendation, three governments
submitted papers on the subject to the Fourth Assembly, each
making an interesting proposal.

Argentina tried to pick up where the Geneva Conference
had left off; it suggested a multilateral agreement that would
leave route negotiations to bilateralism, would require that
all bilateral agreements include a grant of Fifth Freedom,
but would limit Fifth Freedom rather sharply in two ways.
First, an airline would have the right to carry such traffic
up to only a relatively low proportion of the Third/Fourth
Freedom traffic. (Argentina suggested 20 percent.) Secondly,
the fare charged by a long-distance airline for a local journey
could not undercut the fare charged for the same journey by
the airlines of the two neighboring states. [3]

For example, a United States airline flying from New
York to Rio de Janeiro and on to Buenos Aires could not
charge a passenger traveling only between the latter two
points a fare lower than that charged by the Argentinian and
Brazilian carriers between the same points. This differed
from the proposal made at Chicago to permit a fare differential
whereby the Fifth Freedom passenger would be charged more
than if he took the same trip on an airline whereon he would
be Third or Fourth Freedom traffic. It would, however,
have permitted Argentina and Brazil (to continue the above
example) to decide between them on a rate floor, and to maintain this floor, for traffic for which they naturally felt they
had a primary interest by comparison with that of a long-
distance carrier not of either's nationality.

This latter proposal is illustrative not only of the obvious
fear that large, well-equipped, well-known airlines would
offer a strong attraction even to local passengers; it also

reflects a feeling that traffic between one's own country and an immediately neighboring country is more peculiarly the "property" of the two contiguous states than traffic between one's own country and more distant points. The latter feeling (and it can scarcely be called anything more than that) exists also in situations where there is no question of a disparity in the equipment or reputations of the competing airlines. For example, to this day the United Kingdom and France will not permit United States airlines to carry local traffic between London and Paris.

The other two papers submitted originated with the United Kingdom and New Zealand. Departing substantially from the line of negotiation developed through Bermuda and Geneva, both of these governments raised again the question of the ownership of an airline by an international organization and the operation by it of the world's trunk routes. The suggestion was not surprising in the case of New Zealand since it, jointly with Australia, had submitted and defended such a plan at the Chicago Conference in 1944. It may, however, seem a somewhat surprising step for the United Kingdom until it is recalled that the Labour Party had prepared such a position prior to the Chicago Conference but was not in a position to implement it since it was then the opposition party. But by 1950, at the time of the Fourth ICAO Assembly, there was a Labour Government in London.

Both papers advocated a study of the pooling of flight schedules, passenger handling facilities, and revenues among the various airlines over particular routes, and in particular areas, to be followed by a series of future steps as experience grew, leading toward an international organization for each area and, ultimately, a single operating organization for all of the world's trunk routes. [4]

The Fourth Assembly gave rather scant attention to the far-reaching scheme of the United Kingdom and New Zealand. Its Economic Commission (operating as a committee of the whole of the Assembly) voted that the Council should discontinue work on the concept of joint ownership and operation but that it might "continue to receive whatever data was available from States with experience in this field." The Assembly adopted a resolution to this effect. [5] The paper submitted by Argentina likewise received no particular attention.

Both the Economic Commission and the Assembly agreed with the view of the Council that there be no discussion of substantive issues, and there was none. The Assembly, however, took a somewhat more positive step with respect to the general question of the multilateral agreement than the Council had taken. It found that the replies collected from the various members by the Council since the Second Assembly "reflect a continuing desire for a multilateral agreement, but nevertheless are insufficient in number and in most cases inadequate in substance." The Assembly urged the members to comply fully with the request that had been made two years before, and to do so by April 1, 1951, after which the Council was "to recommend, in due time, what further action should be taken in this matter."[6]

In the midst of this indifference, one significant discussion took place within the Economic Commission. The view was expressed by some delegates (though not a majority) that, instead of pursuing the concept of a single, worldwide, multilateral agreement, it would be preferable to attempt to arrange meetings of groups of states by regions wherever the climate seemed favorable for the multilateral approach.[7] Three years later, as will be seen, this was the turn that events took.

The Seventh Assembly

The Fifth and Sixth Assemblies, held respectively in 1951 and 1952, were so-called "limited" sessions, dealing primarily with administrative and budgetary questions, it having been decided at the 1950 session that a full-scale Assembly session was desirable only every third year.[8] Thus, it was not until the Seventh Session in 1953 that questions concerning a multilateral agreement were again considered.

The ICAO Council, meeting prior to this Assembly, had concluded "that there was no immediate prospect of progress toward a universal multilateral agreement." It also found "that the possible partial solutions that had been suggested had not reached a sufficiently advanced stage to justify action by the Organization."[9] (Among the "partial solutions" were multilateral agreements covering a region such as the North Atlantic, or a category of traffic such as cargo or mail.)[10]

Very shortly thereafter, however, the Committee of Ministers of the Council of Europe, by resolution, invited ICAO to call a conference of the Western European states to consider improved cooperation among the European airlines, as well as the possibility of establishing some form of multilateral exchange of commercial rights.[11] The ICAO Council, shortly before the opening of the Assembly, reacted favorably to the suggestion and proposed that a committee be established

to prepare for such a conference. This matter thus lay before
the Assembly as the one positive proposal with respect to
multilateralism.

The Seventh Assembly gave separate consideration to
scheduled and to nonscheduled service, and adopted a separate
resolution for each.

Scheduled Service

The Economic Commission of the Assembly, after extensive discussion, proposed a resolution, subsequently adopted
by the Assembly, which declared "that there is no present
prospect of achieving a universal multilateral agreement, although multilateralism in commercial rights to the greatest
possible extent continues to be an objective of the Organization."
The resolution went on to approve the convening of a European
regional conference as had been suggested by the Council of
Europe. It also recommended that the ICAO Council "keep
under review" possible partial solutions which might lead toward the objective of multilateralism. The vote on the resolution was unanimous in the Economic Commission and was
adopted "in the absence of objections or abstentions" by the
plenary meeting of the Assembly. [12]

It will be apparent at this point that the Seventh Assembly
really took no step forward beyond anything done at the Fourth
Assembly, with the single and noteworthy exception of approv-
ing the European regional conference. As if to underline its
negative view of the prospects of a universal multilateral
agreement, the Assembly in a separate administrative resolution directed the Council "to give first priority" insofar as
economic matters were concerned to a problem altogether
outside the multilateral question--i.e., charges for airports
and for air navigation facilities. This resolution, which dealt
with the selection of subjects for study by the Council in the
economic field, did not even mention a multilateral agreement. [13]

Nonscheduled Service

The resolution with regard to worldwide nonscheduled
air service was every bit as negative as that dealing with the
scheduled service. The Economic Commission considered a
tentative suggestion of the ICAO Council concerning a general
conference to be held in 1954 "to discuss regulations, conditions, and limitations relating to international nonscheduled

operations." This might have opened the way for either a multilateral agreement limited to charter flights or to a multilateral declaration as to desirable practices with regard to such services. The commission, however, decided against the holding of a conference since "there appeared to be little prospect that it would be successful."[14]

The resolution adopted unanimously by the Economic Commission and the Assembly asked member states to inform the Council whether they had accepted a definition demarking scheduled from nonscheduled air service that the Council had adopted in 1952, or, if not, what methods they used to distinguish between the two types of service. (The definition of a "Scheduled International Air Service" is found in ICAO Document 7278.) The member governments were also to inform the Council as to difficulties they might be experiencing in the operation of charter flights and to submit suggestions as to practical steps that might be taken to resolve such problems. The Council, however, was not even instructed to proceed, after receiving comments from the various governments, to the drafting of any agreement or policy statement; instead, it was merely to advise the governments as to practical steps they might take "to facilitate the operation of nonscheduled air transport."

The single accomplishment of any consequence at the Seventh Assembly thus appears to have been with respect to the European regional meeting. In all other respects, the concept of multilateralism not only made no progress but appears to have been firmly shelved.

THE WESTERN EUROPEAN REGIONAL EXPERIENCE

Characteristics of Intra-European Airline Service

Western Europe, which may be defined for civil aviation purposes as all the non-Communist countries of Europe including the British Isles and Turkey, plus Iceland, seems in some respects a highly suitable area for regional efforts in civil aviation cooperation. In terms of politics, standards of living, technological and cultural development, there is a general similarity among these countries. Moreover, since nearly all of them have both the desire and the technological and business acumen to operate a national airline of some consequence, intra-European service is characterized by

relatively numerous airlines for the area involved, with resultant economic problems.

Thus, with an area less than half that of the United
States, and with railroad and highway mileages each only
slightly more than half those of the United States, Western
Europe has air route mileage approximately twice that of the
United States. [15]

While the concentration of population in large cities and
the high degree of cultural and commercial intercourse among
these cities leads to a substantial demand for air service, the
cities are often sufficiently close together so that many intra-
European air services are bedeviled by the "short-haul"
problem.

It is a general principle of transportation economics
that the shorter the haul the higher the per-mile costs. This
is particularly true in air transportation because the costs
of take-off and landing are proportionately higher, by comparison with the costs of merely flying at cruising altitudes,
than are comparable expenses of other modes of commercial
transport such as bus, truck, and railroad. These costs,
when spread over a short flight stage, are obviously far more
burdensome than when spread over a long stage. In the United
States, a special category of airline known as the "local service air carrier," which conducts primarily short-haul services to small cities, continues today to require a direct government subsidy, while the American domestic trunklines have
not received a direct subsidy for many years.

Western European countries have sought to cope with
the short-haul problem partly by subsidizing loss operations
of their carriers and partly by various bilateral capacity
restrictions, pooling arrangements, and other restrictions
designed to so limit service that the load factors will be
relatively high. There is a dilemma which should be mentioned
here: if airlines reduce frequencies, they may find that the
shorter the haul involved the higher the proportion of traffic
they will lose to surface carriers by the reduction in the number of flights. European passenger train service is tradition-
ally good and, if a person wishes to depart at a particular
hour, he will not wait very long for a flight scheduled at a
later hour when a train (or his own automobile) will get him
to his destination nearly as soon or sooner.

Intra-European services as a whole frequently show
losses. For example, a report prepared by an organization
of European airlines called the European Air Research Bureau showed that the intra-European services of the airlines

of Western Europe suffered losses in each year from 1959 to
1962, with the situation worsening each year. In a rapidly
growing business such as air transportation, a continuing and
worsening loss trend seems surprising. The explanation given
by this Bureau is that the number of flights scheduled and the
seats on each aircraft have been increasing at a pace even
greater than an otherwise healthy increase in the number of
passengers. The report implies that the European carriers,
in their zeal to compete, must be careful not to let the amount
of service outrun the demand for it. [16]

Commenting on the short-haul problem, one authority,
using the concept of "seat miles" rather than route miles as
his standard, found that 77 percent of seat mileage within
Western Europe was on stages of less than 500 miles. [17] The
most fortunate of the intra-European carriers may well be
the British short-haul airline, BEA, whose routes for the
most part involve service across the English Channel, where
the benefit to the passenger from avoiding the train-ship-train
trip gives the airline an increased advantage over its surface
competitors.

There is, of course, a political as well as an economic
argument for increased cooperation in civil aviation among
these countries. The movement toward European political
unity which led to the establishment of the Council of Europe
in 1949 gave rise to discussions within that body of the desirability of tackling the question of regional civil aviation cooperation as one of many facets of political cohesion. There were
at the time over one hundred bilateral agreements among the
countries of Western Europe, a figure which may seem
strangely high until it is observed that the possible number
of such agreements among the nineteen countries is the square
of nineteen, or three hundred sixty-one.

Proposals in the Council of Europe

Even prior to the establishment of the Council of Europe
in 1949, there had been sentiment for having European regional political bodies concern themselves with civil aviation
matters. One authority had urged the earlier political organization called Western Union, made up of Belgium, France,
Luxembourg, the Netherlands, and the United Kingdom, to
seek the establishment of some sort of single European air-
line-operating authority which would be functionally equivalent
to a single airline. He held that there were "much stronger

arguments for a European authority" than could be adduced
in support of a worldwide authority such as that proposed by
Australia and New Zealand at Chicago, and that there was "no
more practical garment with which to begin" the move toward
European political unity than civil aviation. [18]

In 1951, the consultative assembly of the Council of
Europe (a body consisting of members of the parliaments of
the several countries) considered several proposals, notably
the "Bonnefous Plan," the "Sforza Plan," and a recommendation of the consultative assembly's own Committee on Economic
Questions.

The Bonnefous Plan would have established a High Authority for European transport systems (not merely air transport)
along the general lines of the High Authority for the coal and
steel industries which had been established as part of the
European Coal and Steel Community among the six nations
who were later to form the Common Market. Presumably
this would have meant the continued existence of separate
airlines, but subject to a regulatory body with extensive controls over capacity, fares, and routes, and perhaps with
authority to approve or even to direct pooling arrangements
and mergers. [19]

The Sforza Plan, submitted by the Italian Foreign Minister, sought to establish a single authority resembling a
syndicate, in which each state's airline would play a role
determined by such factors as its country's population, geo-
graphical position, and area. The identity of the separate
national airlines would have been maintained, but as subordi-
nate operating units.

A noteworthy feature of the Sforza Plan was that the
cabotage concept would have been applied to all intra-European
air travel. Thus, a United States airline would have been
prohibited from picking up traffic at London or Paris, for
example, and taking it to Rome or Athens. No longer would
such traffic have been classified as Fifth Freedom, but as
cabotage, just as if the whole of Western Europe were one
country.

Such a measure would have caused strong opposition in
the United States, and perhaps in countries such as Israel
and India whose airlines need intra-European traffic to support their long routes from the homeland to the United States.
Yet there is a certain logic to application of the cabotage concept in this manner. If the fifty states of the United States
are construed as roughly paralleling the nineteen states of
Western Europe in area and population, then each area might

be construed as having an equally justified claim to the cabotage prohibition if the latter were, indeed, based on economic
considerations. Perhaps what is really demonstrated here is
that the reservation of cabotage traffic to a country's own airlines is based purely on legal and political considerations.

The third proposal, that of the Committee on Economic
Questions of the Consultative Assembly, favored a single
European body to operate all the intra-European air routes.

The Consultative Assembly, however, watered down these
proposals somewhat in making its recommendation to the
Committee of Ministers of the Council of Europe. It advocated
instead that there be a conference of European government and
airline representatives to consider the founding of "an association of airline companies to take charge of air communications
between member States."

The airlines of Europe strongly opposed these plans. So
also did their governments. The Committee of Ministers of
the Council of Europe, made up of the Foreign Ministers or
their deputies (and thus the governments) of the member
states, declined to accept any of the proposals and, in fact,
did not take any affirmative action until two years later, in
1953. It then accepted the concept of holding a regional civil
aviation conference, but required that no consideration should
be given to a single European airline or syndicate or "High
Authority" for air transport.

Indeed, the Committee of Ministers declined even to call
the conference on its own responsibility. Instead, by resolution of March 19, 1953, it asked ICAO to convene one. This
was the resolution which, as has been seen, was taken up by
the Seventh Assembly of ICAO, resulting in the formal call
for such a conference by that body.

The Strasbourg Conference of 1954

A Preparatory Committee, set up by ICAO, met in the
first two weeks of November, 1953, and drew up an agenda
for a European regional conference. The ICAO Council, ap-
proving this agenda, called the conference, to meet at Strasbourg beginning April 1, 1954. The nineteen Western European states were invited to attend, and all other ICAO states
were invited to participate as observers.[20]

The political situation of the time was reflected in the
fact that ICAO did not specifically invite the two Communist
countries which were then ICAO members, Poland and

Czechoslovakia, while it invited a nonmember of ICAO, West
Germany. The nineteen invited states represented the full
membership at the time of the Council of Europe (fourteen),
plus Austria, Finland, Portugal, Spain, and Switzerland.
(Austria and Switzerland have since become members of the
Council of Europe.)

The Strasbourg Conference, officially entitled the Conference on Coordination of Air Transport in Europe, met in
the latter part of April, 1954, in the Assembly Chamber of
the Council of Europe. It was convened by the President of
the ICAO Council, but it subsequently elected its own President.

Its chief accomplishment was the establishment of a
permanent regional organization called the European Civil
Aviation Conference (ECAC). Other than this one achievement,
its work consisted largely of failing to find any basis for a
regional multilateral agreement for scheduled services, even
one continuing to permit bilateral route exchanges, although
it made some positive recommendations as to possible multilateral agreements for all-cargo and nonscheduled flights,
and as to cooperative working arrangements among the European airlines.[21]

One authority describes the conference as characterized
by--

> ...the usual differences of opinion; the Scandi-
> navian countries at one extreme favored a general
> multilateral agreement according European carriers
> complete freedom of operation within Europe; Spain,
> Italy, and France at the other extreme favored a
> cautious approach moving gradually from bilateral-
> ism with carefully devised safeguards against exces-
> sive competition or serious damage to the interests
> of carriers in relatively weak economic positions.[22]

While the Conference was unable to arrive at terms for
an agreement, it nevertheless took an official position in
favor of further efforts to achieve one. Thus, just as the
world conferences and ICAO meetings had repeatedly failed
to achieve a worldwide multilateral agreement, and had as
repeatedly issued statements favoring one in principle, the
Strasbourg Conference came to a similar conclusion of failure-
plus-hope-for-the-future.

The recommendation for future efforts does, however,
set forth certain guidelines. It envisages the indefinite

continuation of bilateral route exchanges, but favors the
gradual reduction of capacity and frequency restrictions,
particularly Fifth Freedom restrictions, for intra-European
traffic. It urges that any multilateral agreement look with
favor upon cooperative working arrangements among the airlines. [23]

The Conference attempted to take a forward step with respect to scheduled all-cargo service. Most scheduled flights
are passenger flights, carrying some cargo and mail in a
separate compartment along with passenger baggage. However, some scheduled flights are designated for cargo only.
For such flights the Conference recommended that the member governments abolish all capacity and Fifth Freedom restrictions for an experimental period of five years, to begin
October 1, 1954. [24] This was, of course, a recommendation
rather than an agreement. It was not generally implemented
and was never made into the form of an agreement.

At the time of the Strasbourg Conference, the number of
all-cargo flights within Europe was small, and the recommendation of the Conference thus was of little moment insofar
as the overall European air transport picture was concerned.
However, had it been widely adopted, it would be of growing
value today as all-cargo service expands. It might also have
given at least some small encouragement to the multilateral
concept in general.

Another recommendation at Strasbourg, and one which
ultimately has achieved a worthwhile result in the form of an
international agreement, had to do with nonscheduled services--
i. e. , with charter flights.

The charter flight, including services where a tour
operator charters an aircraft and sells space on it to the
general public, has developed within Europe particularly in
connection with vacation resorts in the Mediterranean area,
bringing traffic from northern Europe. Article 5 of the Chicago Convention, as has been seen, granted with one hand
what seemed to be a broad opening of the skies of the world
to charter flights, then with the other hand took away what it
had granted by allowing each state to impose such conditions
and limitations on such flights as it saw fit.

The Strasbourg Conference recommended a code relieving
certain categories of intra-European charter flights from
various "conditions and limitations" which would otherwise be
allowed under Chicago Article 5. It invited each European
government to announce its acceptance of the code as an
interim policy until a formal multilateral agreement for

European nonscheduled service could be concluded.   And it
recommended that the ICAO Council and the newly established
European Civil Aviation Conference (ECAC) prepare a draft
of such an agreement. [25]

European Multilateral Agreement
on Nonscheduled Service

The draft agreement was prepared and, in 1955, was
circulated among the nineteen governments who were shortly
to meet for the first plenary session of ECAC. [26]   Its provisions generally followed those of the recommended interim
code.   The plenary session, meeting in late 1955, approved
this draft with minor revisions and recommended to ICAO
that the agreement be opened for signature on April 30, 1956. [27]
Meeting again in a special session on April 26, 1956, the
ECAC members made some further changes in the draft, and,
on April 30, four of them--Belgium, France, Luxembourg,
and Switzerland--signed the document.   Ireland, West Germany,
and the Netherlands signed a few weeks later.   By early 1961,
every ECAC state except Greece had ratified or adhered to the
agreement. [28]   As of 1969, Greece had still not adhered.

Major Provisions of the Agreement

The Multilateral Agreement on Commercial Rights of
Nonscheduled Air Services in Europe establishes a classification of different types of nonscheduled commercial flights.
The multilateral grant of rights varies with the type of charter.
The grant of rights may be broken down into three categories. [29]
Flights in the first category may be operated without need
for obtaining prior approval of the other government or governments.   In this category are flights to meet humanitarian or
emergency needs, occasional flights with very small aircraft
(not over six seats), flights where a single person or firm
charters the entire aircraft to move his own staff or merchan-
dise, and an extremely limited number of nonscheduled
flights of any kind.   This last item is of the "catch-all" variety;
its chief feature is a severe numerical limitation of one flight
a month between any pair of points by any one operator.
In the second category there is a grant of similar rights
to all-cargo charter flights and to those passenger charter
flights which are "between regions which have no reasonably
direct connection by scheduled air services"; but, while prior
permission for each flight is not required, any state may step

in at any time and prohibit continuation of services of these
two sorts upon a finding, in its own judgment, that the services
are "harmful to the interests of its scheduled air services."
Furthermore, the apparently broad grant of rights for passenger flights between regions lacking reasonably direct scheduled air service is subject to a sweeping right of any state to
"determine freely the extent of the regions," and to determine
whether they do or do not lack reasonably direct scheduled
service.

Anent the third category there is really no grant of any
operating rights at all. There is simply the statement that,
for nonscheduled services not covered in the first two categories, each state shall publish regulations as to the procedures to be followed where an airline wishes to operate
such a flight, shall accept applications from the airline to the
aviation authorities without need for use of diplomatic channels, and shall not require filing of a request on longer notice
than two business days prior to the flight, except in the case
of an extensive series of flights covered by one application,
where longer notification periods may be specified.

The phrasing of the language for this third category
(Article 3 of the Agreement) required an accommodation of
two different interpretations of Article 5 of the Chicago Convention. That Article, as has been noted, grants rights for
commercial nonscheduled operations, but subjects the grant
to such "regulations, conditions, or limitations" as each state
may impose.

The prevailing interpretation and practice (including that
of the United States) is that a government may require that a
permit be sought for every flight and that it is discretionary
with each government as to whether each permit shall be
granted. In short, the prevailing view is that Chicago Article
5 grants nothing at all, but that it may have a persuasive effect on the signatory governments to refrain from barring
nonscheduled flights altogether. *

Certain governments (notably the Netherlands) challenge

_____

* In practice, the United States and the other major aviation states permit scheduled foreign airlines to conduct charters, both on-route and off-route. Also, some carriers which
specialize in charters are granted basic, continuing authority
by foreign governments to perform charters. These authori-
zations, however, are issued as a matter of discretion based
on reciprocity, and do not derive from any obligation acknowledged by the governments under Chicago Article 5.

this approach, however, and interpret the Chicago Article as
requiring that commercial nonscheduled services be admitted
without the obtaining of prior permission, subject only to
reasonable regulations by the foreign government. This disagreement in interpretation of the Chicago Article was finessed
in Article 3 of the instant agreement by language referring to
procedures for furnishing of information concerning a proposed
flight (a right of the foreign government which is not disputed)
and by adding the phraseology "(with a request for prior permission if one is required)."

The agreement provides for binding arbitration, with the
sanction that any state failing to comply with the decision of
an arbitral tribunal would lose for its airlines all rights
granted under the agreement. The arbitration language provides, first, for an ad hoc tribunal to be set up by the two
disputant states or, failing agreement on this procedure, a
reference to the Council of ICAO for decision. If the Council
should be unwilling to hear the dispute, recourse could then
be had by any disputant to the International Court of Justice.

Weaknesses of the Agreement

One noteworthy feature of the agreement is that it grants
virtually no rights whatever with respect to the two most
numerous and important types of intra-European nonscheduled
flights: the "affinity" charter and the "inclusive tour" charter.
The first of these involves the chartering of the aircraft
by an organization such as a fraternal or social club, profes-
sional association, or the employees of one corporation or
students of one university, with the costs of the charter prorated among the participants. The second type involves the
chartering of the aircraft by a tour operator and the filling of
the seats with participants in "package" tours. The latter
type has been particularly common for the carriage of traffic
from Scandinavia, Germany, and the British Isles to Mediterranean resorts. Neither type is granted any rights by the
multilateral agreement except the one-a-month grant under
the "catch-all" provision of the first category discussed above,
and the "right" (if it can be called that) to file permit applications as near as two days to the flight departure date and
without need to use diplomatic channels. *

---

* These two types of charter, if they happened to be
"between regions which have no reasonably direct connection
by scheduled air services," would also have the limited rights

In short, the substantial programs of affinity and inclusive
tour charters which the European carriers conduct must proceed largely upon the insecure basis of the seeking of a permit for each flight (or each series of flights for one charterer),
subject to grant or denial on a case-by-case basis in the complete discretion of each government. Thus, even with the
multilateral agreement in force, these important categories
of charter flights within Europe do not have as much right to
operate as do the scheduled services; lacking an effective
multilateral grant, they are also not covered by intergovernmental bilateral agreements as are the scheduled services.
The anomaly here is, of course, that ICAO, as has been seen,
had singled out nonscheduled service as a more ready subject
for broad grant of rights than the scheduled services.

Subsequent Recommendations on Nonscheduled Service

In 1961, however, at the Fourth Plenary Session of ECAC,
a recommendation was approved whereby the governments
were urged to permit the affinity type of charter up to four
flights in any two successive months by any one operator or
group of operators between any pair of points, subject to ex
post facto termination if any government found the service
harmful to its scheduled airline operations. [30]
It should be noted that this provision for affinity charters
was not presented as a proposed amendment to the multilateral
agreement. The fourth session of ECAC concluded that it
should be left in the form of a recommendation, but that if the
recommended practice proved "generally acceptable and useful," consideration could later be given to putting the substance
of the recommendation into the agreement. [31] However, the
agreement has not been amended to incorporate any liberal-
ized treatment of the affinity charter, nor in any other respect,
as of 1969.
On the matter of inclusive tour charters, the ECAC session merely recommended that the member states "should
continue to adopt a liberal attitude towards flights exclusively
reserved for inclusive tours." The statement recognized,
however, that such tours enabled persons to travel who otherwise could not afford regular air fares, that there was a
"social value" in such a result, and that tour charters might

---

described above under this language (Article 2 (2)), subject
to the sweeping rights of the governments to limit or prohibit.

help rather than hurt scheduled service in the long run by
establishing passenger habits of air travel. [32]

To conclude, then, the discussion of the nonscheduled
agreement, it may be stated that this sole existing example
of a multilateral agreement (in the sense of this study) has
proved a relatively puny experiment in multilateralism.

Other European Regional Developments

A Multilateral Agreement for Scheduled Services

The first meeting of ECAC in 1955 followed the lead of
the Strasbourg Conference by concluding, after some discussion, that "it would be premature to attempt to develop a
multilateral agreement" on scheduled service within Europe. [33]
At the Second Plenary Session of ECAC in 1957, there was
more discussion, but it was inconclusive. [34] The question
since that time has not been seriously considered.

There has, however, been a trend toward "pooling,"
wherein carriers not only jointly plan schedules but actually
apportion the income earned in each market. Such devices
can be looked upon as a "back door" approach to multilateralism. They can also be criticized as yielding monopoly-like
conditions whereby, in light of the income-apportioning arrangement, an airline can with impunity be indifferent to its
customers' interests. Describing and defending such pooling,
one writer holds that it "will stimulate a process of joint ex-
ploitation even to the point of the creation of a European air
carriage association--a supranational international partner-
ship. "[35]

The European Common Market and "Air Union"

The Treaty of Rome, which established the European
Common Market, touches very lightly on air transport. It is
left to be provided for, if at all, by future action of the Council
of Ministers, and all decisions respecting it must be by a
unanimous vote of the Ministers (Article 84 (2) of the Rome
Treaty). [36] Thus, despite the strong economic ties among the
six members of the Common Market, the airlines of these
nations remain outside the Common Market pattern. There
has been no move toward a single airline to bear the flag, so
to speak, of the Six, either for services within the Six or for
services between them and the outside world.

A development in the late 1950's and early 1960's, related
to the Common Market but outside its framework, was the
"Air Union" proposal. This was a plan set forth by the French
airline, Air France, in 1957, bearing the name "Europair,"
subsequently changed to "Air Union." It was to have been a
far-reaching pooling agreement among the flag airlines of the
Six except Luxembourg which, having only a very small airline, was not included. Each airline would continue to own
and operate its fleet of aircraft, using its own crews and in-
signia, but all flights would operate under a single scheduling
arrangement and there would be a pooling of both revenues
and expenses in accordance with a quota established in the
agreement. This arrangement was described by The Economist
as a "half-way house" between the usual type of pooling and
total integration into a single airline. [37]

It should be emphasized that this plan was not intended to
apply to intra-European services at all, but only to services
between the cities of the five countries, on the one hand, and
points in the rest of the world, on the other hand--i. e., the
long-haul international routes of these airlines.

After long negotiations, a charter was drawn up in 1961.
There were delays in obtaining the approvals of the several
governments, France insisting on representation of the
governmental administrations, not merely the airlines, on
the governing board. There was extreme difficulty in agreeing
on the size of the "quota" of service each airline was to have
and, as negotiations went on from year to year, the respective
strengths of the airlines changed. The German and Italian
airlines expanded their services faster than the others and
consequently began insisting on larger quotas.

An additional problem was a change of heart by the
Netherlands airline, KLM, and its withdrawal from the proposed union. Subsequently, the remaining airlines disagreed
as to future orders of the supersonic aircraft, which are expected to begin service in the 1970's and had to be ordered
many years in advance. Certain of them ordered the Anglo-
French Concorde, while others ordered the American supersonic aircraft. A commitment of such long range to equip
with different types of aircraft indicated that the carriers
were not thinking along lines of comparability of their fleets.
Comparability of engines and spare parts, as well as of maintenance and overhaul facilities and procedures, is at the heart
of any far-reaching pooling arrangement.

By the middle sixties, the Air Union concept seemed to
fade away, and nothing much has been heard of it for quite
some time.

More recently, the idea has been advanced that certain general provisions of the Treaty of Rome might be applied to airline service within the six member states--such as prohibitions on subsidies or concerted practices which "distort competition." One writer suggests that there may be mergers among the airlines of the Six that will cut across lines of nationality, consistent with the philosophy of the treaty respecting freedom of financial participation and worker movement. But he holds also that the open competition generally espoused by the treaty cannot be applied in toto to air transportation; supervision would be necessary, either by "one or more Community Institutions or [by] a special authority attached to them."[38]

ATTITUDES TOWARD A WORLDWIDE MULTILATERAL AGREEMENT, 1953-69

There has been no progress made toward any type of worldwide multilateral agreement during the sixteen years from 1953 to 1969. What interest there was in the early years of this period seems to have diminished as time has gone on.

In the United States, for example, the interdepartmental committee charged with coordinating American aviation policy declared in 1954 that the ultimate objective of the United States "has been and continues to be the achievement of a multilateral air transport agreement."[39] Yet by 1959, one United States official could say that the airline industry had become more and more "national" and that "it seems difficult to conceive of a multilateral air transport agreement which would be acceptable to American interests in the foreseeable future."[40] The "American interests" referred to by him, however, are equated with the protection and promotion of the United States international air carriers; the present study will take a broader view of what constitute the interests of the American people.

In 1963, an Interagency Steering Committee took the position, in a report on international air transport issued with presidential approval, that:

The U.S. will maintain the present framework of bilateral agreements by which air routes are exchanged among nations and the rights to carry traffic on them are determined according to certain broad principles. The substitution of a multilateral agreement seems even less feasible or acceptable today

than when first attempted at the Chicago Conference
of 1944.[41]

This report was the product of extensive research over an
eighteen-month period, in which the government agencies
were assisted by two private research firms and consulted
with the United States airlines.[42] As of 1969, there has been
no subsequent statement of an American position. Thus it
can be concluded that the United States position on a multilateral agreement is clearly and flatly negative.

As another example of complete lack of progress, the
Council of ICAO in 1955 took a position favoring the drafting
of two worldwide multilateral treaties, one for cargo flights,
and one for the carriage of mail, but nothing has come of
these recommendations.[43]

The absence of progress toward multilateralism should
be viewed in conjunction with the great increase, between
1953 and 1969, in international airline traffic, as well as in
the number of airlines serving such traffic, and the number
of countries interested in having airlines in international
services. The importance of air transport to the world, as
well as the complexity of the problems and the possibilities
of political obstruction to good air service, have all grown
during the period. The need for greater international cooperation in this field grows apace while the achievement of such
cooperation stagnates.

In the concluding chapter the the several proposals discussed in this chapter will be evaluated to see if one or more
of them might form the basis for an attempt, in the present
era, to achieve a greater degree of international cooperation.
Particular attention will be focused on the 1946 Draft as the
closest approach to an ideal construction of multilateralism
in this field. However, it will also be noted that the prospects
for obtaining consent of the governments to so far-reaching an
agreement seem so dim that perhaps attention should be focused
on a multilateral pact wherein the bilateral system is retained,
such as the Minority Draft drawn up in 1947 or the similar
Geneva Conference Draft drawn up later that same year.

NOTES

1. Resolution A2-16, cited in ICAO Document 7017, p.
10; Ivor Thomas, "Civil Aviation--International Questions
Outstanding," International Affairs, 25:56-65, 1949.

2. ICAO Document 7148, p. 48.

3. ICAO Document 7225, pp. 380-91.

4. ICAO Document 7225, pp. 392-431.

5. Ibid., pp. 254-5 and 345.

6. Ibid., pp. 343-4.

7. Ibid., p. 253.

8. Jacob Schenkman, International Civil Aviation Organization (Geneva: Librairie E. Droz, 1955), p. 147.

9. ICAO Document 7456, p. 31.

10. Edward M. Weld, "ICAO and the Major Problems of International Air Transport," Journal of Air Law and Commerce, 20:457, 1953.

11. ICAO Document 7456, p. 31.

12. ICAO Documents 7409, p. 67, 7415, p. 6, and 7417, pp. 27-8.

13. ICAO Documents 7415, p. 5, and 7417, p. 27.

14. ICAO Documents 7415, pp. 8-9, and 7417, p. 28.

15. Stephen Wheatcroft, The Economics of European Air Transport (Cambridge: Harvard University Press, 1956), p. 7.

16. ICAO Working Paper ECAC/5-WP/45, July 5, 1964.

17. Wheatcroft, op. cit., p. 40.

18. Ivor Thomas, op. cit., p. 65.

19. Material on the Bonnefous and other plans, and on the actions within the Council of Europe, is derived from the following sources: H.A. Wassenbergh, Post-War Civil Aviation Policy and the Law of the Air (second edition; The Hague: Martinus Nijhoff, 1962), pp. 79-82; "European Civil Aviation Conference," Journal of Air Law and Commerce, 28:78 and 94,

1961; D. Goedhuis, "The Role of Air Transport in European Integration," Journal of Air Law and Commerce, 24:273-85, 1957.

20. ICAO Document 7456, p. 31.

21. The full text of the recommendations of the Confer- ence appears in J. G. Gazdik, "Conference on the Co-ordi- nation of Air Transport in Europe--Strasbourg--April 21- May 8, 1954," Journal of Air Law and Commerce, 21:330-8, 1954.

22. Ibid., p. 330.

23. Recommendation 2 of the Conference, Ibid., p. 332.

24. Recommendation 3 of the Conference, Ibid., p. 332.

25. Recommendations 5 and 6 of the Conference, Ibid., pp. 333-4.

26. ICAO Document ECAC/1/WP/2, August 16, 1955.

27. ICAO Document ECAC/1/WP/61, December 17, 1955, pp. 18 and 39.

28. Wassenbergh, op. cit., p. 95.

29. ICAO Document 7695 contains the full text of this Agreement.

30. ICAO Document 8185, p. 13.

31. Ibid., p. 9.

32. Ibid., p. 15.

33. ICAO Document 7676, cited in Wassenbergh, op. cit., p. 93.

34. ICAO Document 7799, cited in Wassenbergh, op. cit., p. 175.

35. Michel Pourcelet, "The International Element in Air Transportation," Journal of Air Law and Commerce, 33:79, 1967.

36. Treaty Establishing the European Economic Community, (Brussels: Publishing Services of the European Communities, 1961), p. 74.

37. "Can Air Union Get Airborne?" The Economist, (August 4, 1962), p. 459.

38. Dr. Wolfgang Stabenow, "The International Factors in Air Transport Under the Treaty Establishing the European Economic Community," Journal of Air Law and Commerce, 33:117-31, 1967.

39. United States Air Coordinating Committee, Report of the Air Coordinating Committee on Civil Air Policy (Washington: Government Printing Office, 1954), p. 35.

40. Albert W. Stoffel, "American Bilateral Air Transport Agreements on the Threshold of the Jet Transport Age," Journal of Air Law and Commerce, 26:120 and 122, 1959.

41. "Statement on International Air Transport Policy," (Washington: The White House, April 24, 1963), p. 7. (Mimeographed.)

42. G. Griffith Johnson, "The International Aviation Policy of the United States," Journal of Air Law and Commerce, 29:366, 1963.

43. Wassenbergh, op. cit., p. 88.

4

ANALYSIS
OF
NATIONAL AVIATION
INTERESTS

This chapter will be concerned with the motives and objectives of governments in establishing and promoting their
airlines, and with what the motives and objectives ought properly to be.

There is no ideal way in which to subdivide this rather
broad topic, and the subdivision to be used here is necessarily
arbitrary. For purposes of analysis, three major headings
will be used: Prestige and other psychological considerations;
economic considerations; and political (including military) considerations.

There will unavoidably be some arbitrary designations
such as, for example, treating under the heading of "prestige"
the concept that "trade follows the flag," even though the idea
has obvious economic implications. Similarly, the desire to
promote aircraft manufacturing will be considered as "economic"
although it is also of political importance to the extent that manufacture of civil aircraft establishes a base convertible to manufacture of military aircraft.

Throughout the analysis, attention will be focused on states
with large traffic-generating potential versus those with small
potential, states with substantial aircraft manufacturing versus
those with little or no such manufacturing, and the particular
position of the less developed countries, the latter being sub-
divided in turn into those with international airlines (e.g., India
and many Latin American countries) and those with no such
services.*

---

*The term "less developed countries," abbreviated as

PSYCHOLOGICAL CONSIDERATIONS

Prestige

That an international airline gives some kind of status or prestige to its country is a concept frequently asserted in the literature of aviation, but difficult to prove. The term "prestige" might be defined as the opinion which the world holds of the airline's country, the respect in which the nation is held, either in a general sense or in a specific sense as for its technological achievements.

The Soviet Union, for example, may promote its airline in the hope that the peoples of the world, seeing it (and the Soviet-manufactured aircraft it employs), will be impressed not only with Soviet technology but with the ideology of the system. Japan and India may hope that their ability to operate safe, efficient airlines (albeit with aircraft manufactured elsewhere) will contribute toward persuading the world of the soundness of their industrial products. Some governments may even hope that the existence of an international airline will in some manner give them added political weight in their relationships with other governments.

Yet it would seem that, with airlines now become commonplace throughout the world, there is ever-diminishing validity in the reference by one authority in 1942 to "the deep impression which flying makes on man's imagination everywhere," and his statement that "travel by air still has a spectacular quality that compels attention."[1]

The expression "trade follows the flag" may be true enough in the sense that trade follows colonization or the establishment of ocean or air service to a point previously without service. But it seems doubtful that the sheer prestige effect of flying one's airline into another country will be likely today to promote trade with that country. Austria, for example, began a transatlantic airline service in 1969, although good service between Austria and the United States has been offered for many years by airlines of other nationalities. There seems little likelihood that the appearance from day to day at American airports of an Austrian airline will result in promotion of trade or, for that matter, in any change whatever in the opinion

---

"LDCs," will be used herein to refer to countries with low per capita income, often also called underdeveloped or developing countries.

Americans hold of Austria. Airline service is simply not the remarkable event that it was in its earlier years.

It is conceivable that a small new country such as one of the African republics might seek to assert its independence by the establishment of air service to Europe or North America. It would be handicapped by thin traffic and would very likely develop only a small, nonprestigious airline. Furthermore, it would not proclaim technological advancement to the world since it would, of necessity, use aircraft manufactured in another country.

Indicative that many of the new African republics are not succumbing to the prestige concept is the founding of Air Afrique, a consortium established by treaty among eleven African republics, each holding an equal share in ownership, while two French airlines hold minority shares. The consortium is intended to operate service between the eleven countries and the rest of the world.[2] As of 1969, its service to the United States is a pro forma one wherein it tickets passengers, then places them on flights of the United States carrier, Pan American World Airways, from which it has purchased blocks of seats. (This is intended as a temporary arrangement until Air Afrique can conduct its own services to the United States.)[3] The noteworthy fact about the consortium is that it subordinates the nationalistic concept of prestige to practical economics.

The argument that prestige results from the establishment of air service may seem buttressed by the efforts on the part of Germany and Italy in the days of the Axis to penetrate Latin America. Both established airline service across the South Atlantic to South America, while the Germans sought to control, and for a time did control, certain domestic Latin American lines. It is commonly assumed that these activities had a prestige or "propaganda" value, but this is a conclusion difficult to evaluate. If, in fact, such was the result, it does not mean that there would be any such effects from similar activities today, when the world is crisscrossed by airline services.

If much credence is to be given to the prestige idea, it would be necessary to believe, for example, that the world's opinion of Sweden had been lowered, that country's "image" injured, and its identity somehow or other submerged by the fact that its international air services are conducted by a consortium that combines the efforts of Norway, Sweden, and Denmark into Scandinavian Airlines System, functioning for all practical purposes as a single airline. Such a conclusion seems inconceivable. Indeed, it may be questioned whether many persons other than those connected directly with airline

service (or constant transatlantic travelers) can even name
those countries whose airlines have transatlantic service.

It is possible that the prestige concept to some extent
really masks an irrational human feeling wherein a nation is
personified and is considered to be entitled to an international
airline as part of its "personality." The anthropomorphic approach appears often enough in man's thinking about the nature
of the state; there is no reason to suppose that it does not enter
into human thought about international airline service.

Other Psychological Considerations

In the early days of aviation, when the transoceanic routes
were first being established, it may well be that a close look
at the human motivations that underlay such pioneering efforts
would have revealed sheer fascination with this new vehicle,
the challenge to initiate something that had never been done
before, and perhaps something akin to the well-known motivation for climbing Mount Everest: "because it's there."

Such impulses would seem of diminished significance today, yet they cannot be entirely neglected. They may enter
particularly into decisions with respect to notably different
technological steps such as the supersonic transport.

Consideration also has to be given to what might be called
the psychological results of airline service. The pre-World
War II air routes of the major European powers were particularly directed to their colonies. This will be elaborated on
under the "political" heading herein; however, it is worth noting, as a psychological consideration, that the existence of
air service placing the mother country a few days (rather than
weeks) away from the colony was thought to give a feeling of
a closer bond between the two. Whatever reasons led to the
dissolution of the colonial empires, the absence of good air
service to the mother country was not one of them, inasmuch
as highly subsidized services of this sort were a dominant
feature of the world's air-route map as early as the 1930's.[4]

Another result of the establishment of international airline
service which might be designated "psychological" is the building up of national self-confidence. Thus, a less developed
country (LDC) that accomplishes what may for it be the difficult
task of founding an international airline may be encouraged by
this success to try other difficult tasks. Conversely, of course,
an unsuccessful airline service (premised, perhaps, on prestige rather than economics) might discourage the nation from

other difficult tasks. The currently important question of the
LDC in international airline service will be covered in greater
detail in the section on economic considerations.

Other psychological results of international airline service
have to do with the utility of transportation of any kind. Travel
per se lends variety and depth to people's lives, and is found
by most people to be inherently enjoyable. The ability to travel
widely has the result (aside from its political and economic
implications which will be discussed later) of satisfying sheer
human curiosity as to distant places and cultures. Indeed, one
of the basic texts in transportation refers to ". . . quick, inexpensive, and confortable transportation of passengers which
may yield as real a pleasure to those who take advantage of it
as that derived from the contemplation of art or the consump-
tion of much-prized material goods."[5]

If it be assumed that an ultimate objective of any government is, or ought to be, the happiness of its citizens or the
promotion of their right (in Jefferson's phrase) to the "pursuit
of happiness," it may well be that this aspect deserves more
attention than it generally receives from governments intent
upon the pursuit of the more obvious political and economic
goals of international airline service.

ECONOMIC CONSIDERATIONS

This section will be divided into three types of economic
interest that states have in airline service. The first two are
the rather obvious ones of (1) the earnings of the national airline itself and (2) the impetus given by the national airline to
aircraft manufacturing. The third category is a more general
one wherein, under the heading "Facilitation and Promotion of
National Economies and the World Economy," consideration
will be given to the economic importance of such services as
transportation of tourists, businessmen, mail, and freight.

The Economic Value of the Airline Operation Per Se

As with any economic undertaking, an airline is of importance to a country by reason of its employment of nationals of
that country, of its purchase of such things as aircraft, food,
fuel, and advertising, and by reason of the profits which it pays
to its owners, whether they be private persons or government
entities.

From this limited standpoint, international services of
the airlines of the major powers tend to be relatively unimpor-
tant as proportions of the total economy. Thus, the international services of all United States airlines in 1966 showed
gross revenues of $1,561,321,000, while the Gross National
Product was $752,000,000,000.[6] However, airline revenues
in international services may loom larger in importance where
the country is having problems with its balance of payments
as are both the United States and the United Kingdom at the
present writing. The British carriers, BOAC and BEA, are
of particular significance in balance-of-payments considerations
since they earn about two-thirds of their revenues from foreign
sources.[7]

The airline as a fact of economic importance receives far
more attention in those countries where a relatively large international airline has been established by comparison with
the size and traffic potential of the country itself. Notable
examples of this are the Netherlands airline, KLM, the airline
of Switzerland, Swissair, the Belgian carrier, Sabena, and
the consortium carrier of the three Scandinavian countries
previously mentioned, Scandinavian Airlines System. These
countries are cited by one source as the outstanding examples
of states which have developed "commercial air fleets far ex-
ceeding their domestic needs" as a means of increasing the
wealth of the state.[8]

All these countries, though small in both area and population, are highly advanced in technology, and they may well be
pressing the development of their airlines because the future
course of aviation, even today, is still partly unknown. One
authority, noting this factor, states: "Therefore it behooves
the small country to participate and perhaps influences the development of civil aviation on the possibility that long-run benefits may be derived."[9] For example, these countries may at
least hope that international aviation will some day be opened
up on the same basis as merchant shipping on the oceans where
the right to trade at any port is, as noted in Chapter 1, virtually universally conceded, on a plane not quite that of customary international law but approaching it through both tradition
and various commercial and maritime treaties.

It should be noted that all the above-mentioned small countries (with the obvious exception of Switzerland) have merchant
fleets of substantial size and importance. Indeed, the three
Scandinavian countries have the largest per capita marine
tonnages in the world.[10] The point need hardly be emphasized
that to these countries the national airline is of substantial

importance in the nation's economy and as a device for earning foreign exchange.

As for the less developed countries (LDCs), their international airline operations are of significance in their economies, but often in a somewhat different manner. No LDC has an international airline comparable in size with the carriers of the small Western European states mentioned above, much less with those of the United States or the United Kingdom, although airlines of Argentina, Brazil, Colombia, India, and Pakistan have extensive world operations.[11]

There comes into play the preference of travelers of the Western world for airlines of technologically advanced countries. Much of this may be sheer bias, especially on the matter of safety. Yet, as a result of this preference, an LDC may find itself hard pressed to run a profitable airline service over long international hauls in competition with the airlines of the advanced countries. It is the LDC airline which will have the empty seats. Its government may have to assist it either by direct subsidy or by placing restrictions of some sort on the frequencies or capacity of the competing airlines. The latter has long been the practice of India, Mexico, and Argentina.

It may well be asked--leaving aside all considerations other than the economic--why a government would wish to promote an international airline of its own in the face of evidence that airlines of other countries, already offering it excellent service to the world, are able to operate more efficiently both in terms of attracting passengers and in terms of the lower costs which result from large-scale operations. A look at the cast of economic thought in the LDCs at the present time may answer this question.

The emphasis in these countries, deriving from a general school of thought associated particularly with the Agentine economist Raul Prebisch, is on industrialization as the only possible cure for their low productivity and low per capita income. It is held that no matter how favorable are the conditions in a country for production of a primary product, the terms of trade for any such product being exchanged on the world market for industrial goods will be increasingly unfavorable, as an inexorable long-term trend. It is held further that the limitation of a country's economy to the production of primary products prevents the development of technological skills and administrative talent. In fact, it is argued, even the means for producing the primary product will remain inefficient unless a strong industrial base is constructed to complement the primary-product sector of the economy.

There seems also to be a belief that industrialization will, among other things, have a psychological effect on the people of a country, transforming a traditional lackadaisical dependence on the production of primary goods by antiquated methods into a setting of higher goals and a working toward their achievement. Transport policy in the LDCs, therefore, as noted in a recent Brookings study, must be clearly linked with the general economic policy as well as with education, health, social welfare, and the redistribution of income, since it has so great an effect on all of these.[12]

Although the operation of an airline is not what is usually thought of, in this context, under the term "industrialization," it seems likely that this type of thinking about economic development would lead in many instances to a determination to establish an airline, even though there might seem little prospect for it to compete on straight, unsubsidized terms with larger, established competitors. There is, in fact, as part of the Prebisch school of thought, a belief that favors the founding of a new industry even where the product would be cheaper to import, if the result is a higher rate of return on capital shifted from a traditional use.[13]

If there be added to this concept the idea that any new industry will contribute to the building up of what Prebisch calls "technological density," then the case becomes stronger for going ahead with the industry--i.e., founding the airline--in the teeth of the more orthodox economic arguments based on comparative advantage. Prebisch defines technological density as "available techniques and skills." He goes on to say:

> The main industrial centres of the world have attained considerable technological density in the course of time; they are not limited to just this or that specialty but have at their disposal a whole complex of specialties and techniques which tends to extend over a growing proportion of the economically active population and which is reflected in a vast range of skills, from the manual worker right up to the senior technician and the alert and capable executive.[14]

The country must, of course, be careful not to enter an industry far beyond its available skills. But, unlike aircraft manufacturing which requires an exceedingly high level of technology and, indeed, a truly advanced managerial sophistication, the operation of an airline is nothing in and of itself beyond the grasp of any country. The aircraft can be purchased from the technologically advanced countries. Flight crews fall, to be sure, in a category of very high skills; but crews can be hired from abroad at the outset until a select small number of one's own citizens can be properly trained, and this training can be received abroad. Typically, a new airline will hire crews of American or European nationality. In some instances they have gone out of their way to advertise this fact to their potential passengers as a means to instill confidence.* The operation of an airline may prove valuable in earning foreign exchange, provided that outpayments of foreign exchange for the purchase and maintenance of aircraft and payments to crews of other nationalities do not offset the foreign exchange earnings.

Such functions as maintenance and overhaul require skilled technicians and mechanics, but such services are available for hire from other airlines. It is commonplace for not only the airlines of the LDCs but many airlines of small advanced countries to have such work done at foreign airports by other airlines, sometimes even by their chief competitors. Unlike other pieces of machinery, the aircraft by its nature is not tied to one locale but is from day to day at various airports around the world where excellent overhaul and maintenance facilities may be for hire. Yet here, as with flight crews, an LDC can, and very likely will, obtain training for a select group of its nationals at a foreign overhaul base and bring them back to perform work on aircraft of the home airline.

The other functions of an airline, far from requiring the talents of a highly industrialized society, may on the contrary lend themselves to a far less sophisticated society. The transport of passengers is a service function which does not lend itself to much mechanization. The servicing of passengers, including the giving of information, the sale of tickets, the handling of baggage, meal service and other amenities aboard the aircraft all would appear to lend themselves particularly well to a society where a meticulous attention to detail, a courteous attitude, and a relatively low wage scale are characteristic. In some respects these aspects of airline operation can be compared with the operation of a cruise ship or hotel.

---

*For example, recent advertisements by Air Jamaica stress Jamaican stewardesses and food and a Jamaican string band, but refer to a contractual arrangement with Air Canada whereby the latter flies the aircraft and performs maintenance; and they conspicuously depict Canadian flight crews. Travel Weekly, (May 27, 1969), p. 21; (June 10, 1969), pp. 25-32.

This, then, is an "industry" which an LDC might be inclined to enter from economic considerations alone, despite
the competitive struggle its airline may face.

In fact, one writer expresses the fear that the LDCs will
develop "tramp" airlines which will wander the earth as does
"tramp" shipping, seeking business where they may. He suggests that the United States protect its airlines from future
competition from this source by discouraging purchase by the
LDCs of large, over-ocean aircraft and encouraging purchase
of short-range, smaller equipment which would be valuable for
air service within the LDC and to its immediate neighbors.[15]
The policies of the Export-Import Bank would be adjusted to
this end.

Vested Interests

Before turning to the economic value of aircraft manufacturing, a word should be said concerning the interests that develop,
once an airline has been established (whether in an LDC or any
country) in keeping the airline going and expanding it. The obvious interest of both operating and managerial personnel in
retaining and expanding their jobs, the interest of stockholders
in the profitability of the airline, the interest where airlines
are partly or wholly owned by the government in profitability
as a state budgetary problem, and the interests of investors
and workers in the various airport facilities that develop around
an airline--all are influential upon a government in preserving
and promoting its airlines.

The Manufacture of Civil Aircraft for Airlines

The manufacture of large jet transports for airline use is
successfully undertaken today only by large countries with an
exceedingly high level of technological advancement. An essential characteristic of any aircraft built for airline use is
low cost of operation. This includes such factors as fuel con-
sumption and the nonstop range possible with a full passenger
load, as well as such important and costly factors as the length
of time the various components will function without need for
repair or overhaul. To make a safe, reliable, comfortable
long-range jet aircraft which will also be a low-cost aircraft
is an achievement which has so far been confined to large,
highly advanced states.

The United States is far and away the leading manufacturer

of aircraft for long-range international airline service. The
Soviet Union produces aircraft for its own substantial internal
and external air services but thus far has not made major in-
roads in the sale of large aircraft abroad. The United Kingdom
has made relatively unsuccessful attempts at the production of
long-range aircraft but is a major producer of medium-range
and short-range models.

France has a smaller, but substantial manufacturing industry and it has combined its resources with those of the
United Kingdom in the production of a supersonic aircraft, the
Concorde, which is expected to be capable of long-range flight
and be in production in the early 1970's. Aircraft of commercial
airline size are also manufactured in Canada, West Germany,
Japan, and the Netherlands.[16] Certain other states have aircraft-manufacturing industries, but their output is limited to
military aircraft and/or to very small aircraft for private or
"air taxi" use. These states are Argentina, Austria, Brazil,
Czechoslovakia, Egypt, India, Indonesia, Israel, Italy, Poland,
Spain, Sweden, Switzerland, and Yugoslavia.

It will be seen that the development of the international
services of a country's airlines as a device to promote the
home aircraft-manufacturing industry does not have much applicability today when there are only a few countries doing the
manufacturing of the appropriate models and when there is
little correlation between the country of manufacture and the
countries of the airlines which use the particular make.

Indeed, there are numerous examples where the international airlines of even the major manufacturing powers have
purchased equipment from other nations in preference to those
of domestic manufacture. American domestic carriers in the
1950's purchased the British-manufactured, medium-range
Viscount in large numbers, and today are equipping with another British medium-range model called the BAC-111. In
turn, the British airline BOAC divides its over-ocean fleet
between the home-manufactured VC-10 and its direct rival
and competitor the American Boeing 707 model. BOAC is
also planning to order two new types of United States aircraft
now in the process of development, one the Lockheed L-1011,
the other the Boeing 747, capable of carrying nearly 350 and
500 passengers, respectively.[17]

Neither the Soviet Union nor the United States has reason
to view the international services of its own airlines as of major
consequence to the promotion of its aircraft manufacturing industry. True, the total operations, both domestic and international, of their airlines constitute an important assist to

their manufacturing. However, in both countries, the domestic air services greatly overshadow the international services of their respective lines.

In the United States, only about one-fourth of all American airline revenues are earned in international services. If this factor is applied, by way of example, to figures of the Boeing Aircraft Co., one of the two leading American manufacturers, only 352 of its commercial planes since inception of jets have been sold (or are on order) for the international services of United States carriers, by contrast to 1057 for American domestic services and 549 for foreign airlines.[18] Thus, it would seem that the fate of American aircraft manufacturing is by no means tied to the promotion of the world routes of American carriers.

In the case of the Soviet Union, available data show that only a small proportion of Aeroflot's total service is to foreign points. Its schedules for February, 1969, for example, show 55 flights a week departing from Moscow for foreign points, while the departures from Moscow for domestic points number about 650 a week.[19]

The two "superpowers," being possessed of the world's two major military machines, undoubtedly have a substantial interest in maintaining and promoting their manufactures of large, long-range aircraft. When designed for airline use, aircraft are not adaptable as fighters or bombers, but they are of great importance for the rapid movement of troops and military cargo. Both governments nurture their manufactures of large (and ever larger) transport aircraft, partly since the same plants and personnel which turn out civil aircraft turn out the same models for direct, immediate use by the military, partly because the planes produced and used by the national airlines will be available in a time of military emergency, and partly because the manufacturing process keeps in being the plant and personnel capable of being stepped up to higher output levels in a major military emergency. The interest also extends to the constant development of advances in such fields as metallurgy and electronics.[20]

The point to be made here, however, is that these matters should be assigned only minor significance with respect to the questions of international airline service with which this study is concerned, because, as indicated above, the international airline services of the United States and the Soviet Union constitute only a relatively small portion of the total custom of their home manufacturing industries.

Facilitation and Promotion of Economic Development

Airlines make a variety of contributions to the economies of each nation and to the world economy. Some of them may seem obvious, yet these are the very aspects that are characteristically neglected by governments in the making of civil aviation policies. Typically, governments look to the political, prestige, and military value of their airlines, and to their economic health as business institutions, while dismissing the benefits of civil aviation to the whole economy of nation and world with perhaps no more than a few platitudes.

Airmail service is a case in point. Taken nowadays entirely for granted, its importance to the world economy is seldom given much thought. A business letter travels from a letter-drop in a building in an American city to the office of its recipient in Europe in the space of a day or two, traversing the Atlantic Ocean at a speed of 600 miles an hour, for a total cost at this writing of only 20 cents. Alternate forms of communication, the telephone and telegraph, are much more expensive, while surface mail is much slower.

Air cargo also has a vital and rapidly growing role in the world economy. Indeed, as massive cargo planes are developed, with consequent lowered air-freight costs, the shipment of goods by air may well become a major determinant of the location of industries. Just as industries once tended to locate along navigable waterways when water transport was the only cheap and simple way of moving freight, and as industries subsequently were located with respect to rail and, later, highway service--witness the development of light industries along the circumferential highways on the perimeters of cities--so plant location in many industries may in the future be determined by the air cargo service pattern.

Already there are developments along this line, one example being the growth of industrial plants right at the Shannon Airport in Ireland. This is an airport built far from any major population center for the earlier purpose of a refueling stop for piston aircraft, which now seeks to offset the great decline in its original function as it is overflown by jet aircraft en route to the major European centers.[21] In effect, Shannon Airport is linking itself with the modern trend in manufacturing whereby various components of a manufactured good may be produced at widely scattered points and assembled into a finished product at yet another point.

As with any type of transportation, a principal effect of air-cargo carriage is to facilitate a better division of labor

within the economy of a nation or in the world economy, as
well as the optimum use of land and capital. Similarly, as
with all forms of transportation, air cargo carriage increases
the sources of supply of many products (i.e., any product that
will either travel by air or be made of component parts that
have traveled by air), with a resultant tendency to increase
competition and promote the lowering and equalizing of prices.

Passenger transportation also has an important impact on
the nature and operation of the national and world economies.
The fact, for example, that executives and technicians of large
corporations can travel quickly and readily to distant points,
makes it much easier for a single manufacturing process to
be properly managed even though its component plants may be
scattered widely in different countries and continents. The
trend to the "international corporation", that spreads its enor-
mous interests about the earth, may well not be an unmixed
blessing--a point outside the scope of this study--but without
international air transportation its development and efficiency
would be impeded.

Nor is this impact limited to the corporation with worldwide plant locations. Today's complex manufactures frequently
involve components manufactured by different corporations,
the assembler of which places his trademark on the finished
product. The assembly of these components from distant locations obviously requires adequate transportation. But in addition, and whether the components move by air or surface, the
air passenger transportation of executives and technicians of
the several separate companies greatly facilitates the process.
It is only necessary to consider the negotiations of intricate
industrial contracts, or the working out of technical incompati-
bilities among the components which must go together into the
finished product, to see that person-to-person contact is of
high importance to the world economy. And such patterns of
industrial development tend to spread technologies and to promote technological advances.

Tourist travel has been noted earlier as a contribution of
airlines to the "pursuit of happiness." It should be cited again
for its economic value to the host countries. Virtually all states
seek to attract tourist trade. It is seen both as an aid to economic development of an LDC, in particular by bringing in
foreign exchange, and as an important contribution to the economy of a highly developed country.

Thus, the countries of Western Europe devote substantial
governmental efforts to the promotion of tourism. The United
States, which lagged in this respect in the past, has been spurred

by its balance-of-payments problem to governmental programs
to attract European tourists. And countries such as Spain and
Greece (which, while European, are nevertheless in border-
line LDC condition) have made truly major efforts to develop
tourism as an important adjunct to economic development.

Mexico is another example. One authority holds that
Mexico's economic development in recent years--making it a
bright spot in an otherwise gloomy picture of Latin American
economic development--is due primarily to the proximity of
the United States with its massive, affluent tourist trade. The
American tourist furnishes Mexico with the economic spur
and foreign exchange with which to develop other sectors of
its economy. [22] Another writer notes that in 1963 tourist ex-
penditures accounted for about 40 percent of Mexico's foreign
income. [23]

The usefulness of air transportation as an integral part
of the industrial and commercial life of nations can conflict
seriously with the narrower concept of the health and growth
of the airlines themselves. This is a conflict which arises in
coping with the problem of "overcapacity."

Overcapacity is a term that arises frequently in studies
of the economics of air transportation, yet it is difficult to define since any attempt to say when capacity becomes overcapacity involves one in a subjective balancing of airline interests versus public interests. It makes little sense to count
the proportion of empty seats (or empty cargo space) carried
throughout the year by the airlines serving a market and to
describe the result pejoratively as the "overcapacity." [24]
This wholly fails to allow for the variations in the amount of
traffic by time of day, day of the week, and time of the year,
nor the even more unpredictable variations deriving from the
obvious (but neglected) fact that passengers and shippers of
cargo demand service on the basis of their own business and
personal interests from moment to moment rather than on the
basis of what space the airline may have available or what
habits of traffic demand best suit the airline's purpose.

A scheduled service offers great advantages to the public;
the price of it is that a scheduled flight must depart either
without a full load (and thereby with "overcapacity") or with a
full load, meaning that in all likelihood one or more passengers or shippers of cargo have been unable to get space on
that flight. There are, of course, ways in which airlines seek
to meet the variations in traffic flow. More flights are scheduled at the busiest times of day; more are scheduled for peak
seasons such as summer on the Atlantic: "extra sections"

are flown--i.e., a second or third aircraft is used as part of
one particular scheduled "flight."

But the provision of aircraft and crew is not a matter pre-
cisely adjustable to the varying demand, even if it were possible to predict the latter with precision. The working hours
of flight crews can be, and are, adjusted to a considerable
degree so that flights are operated at times of day and days
of the week which seek to approximate the traffic. It is not
practical, however, either as a matter of employee morale,
union regulations, or safety regulations affecting crew rest,
to order working hours to meet all the variances in traffic.
Furthermore, an airline could not hope to retain highly skilled
flight crews if it furloughed some of its men in lighter seasons.
In practice, airlines normally employ a crew member on annual salary with additional compensation for each flight hour.
To an extent, this helps with the problem: he remains on the
payroll throughout the year but works more frequently and receives premium pay during the busy season.

A look at the North Atlantic passenger market reveals
dramatically the severity of seasonal fluctuations. Table 1
shows the number of passengers carried on the scheduled
services of all airlines between North America and Europe
in each direction for each month of 1967. Traffic in the most
busy month eastbound (July) is more than four times as great
as in the lightest month, February, and roughly three times
as great as in the other winter months, November through
March. Westbound, the peak month is August and the proportions even more extreme--nearly five times as great as February and well over three times the traffic for each of the
other winter months.

A modern large transport aircraft costs money even when
it is not being used; this is a major problem in operating a
scheduled service, especially in a seasonal market. It rep-
resents an investment on the order of $5-10 million earning
no income during idle periods. Furthermore, there is a large
depreciation factor. An aircraft does not so much "wear out"
as become obsolete for airline use by the emergence of new
models which will have higher passenger preference or lower
cost of operation or both. The machine for which the airline
paid millions of dollars may have to be sold after only a few
years for a depressed price. It will be apparent that the airlines must strive to minimize idle aircraft time, yet, faced
with variations in traffic volume, must have fleets which will
at least approach adequate public service on peak days.

TABLE 1

Passengers Carried by all Airlines
in North Atlantic Market in 1967

Month	Eastbound	Westbound
January....................	107, 597	119, 382
February....................	84, 978	94, 132
March.....................	120, 782	127, 293
April......................	161, 809	159, 338
May.......................	236, 844	221, 385
June......................	313, 714	269, 399
July......................	368, 250	297, 422
August....................	296, 425	448, 153
September.................	257, 260	336, 537
October...................	189, 551	255, 823
November..................	105, 746	141, 872
December..................	138, 517	135, 222
Totals	2, 381, 473	2, 605, 958

Source: World Air Transport Statistics (Montreal: International Air Transport Association, 1967), p. 45.

The sum of all this is that airlines fly, typically, at a
load factor in the vicinity of 50 percent--i.e., the average
flight is only half full. Whether this means that the airlines
should be criticized for a condition of "overcapacity" depends
on the value one attaches to the need for airline earnings versus the proper fulfillment of the vital economic function of
scheduled airline service.

Another conflict that faces every government in making
civil aviation policy is between the promotion of its own national airline or airlines in international services and the
benefits to the world economy and, indeed, to its own citizens
and national economy, of the services offered by foreign airlines. Typically, this conflict is resolved by governments in
favor of promotion of the national airline and, indeed, the
prevailing attitude is that the more traffic that travels on the

national airline and the less on the foreign airline, the better.

This attitude wholly neglects the fact that both the world
economy and one's own citizens may benefit from a choice
among the airlines of several states over a particular route.
A similar situation often occurs in commercial policy-making,
where the fact that trade barriers are subject to bilateral
governmental bargaining (plus the fact that domestic indus-
tries--including airlines--have organized political power) may
cause a government supposedly wedded to the principle of
freer world trade to view as a "concession" the lowering of
a tariff or other barrier--even though such a "concession"
may be enormously beneficial to its own consumer citizens. *

This conflict is largely ignored in the literature of air
transportation; even when it is recognized, there is a certain
ambivalence of approach. For example, in the Presidential
"Statement on International Air Transport Policy" issued in
1963 there appears only one sentence which even hints that
American consumers may have an interest in service by
foreign airlines: "The demand for swift, safe passage, not
forced flag flying, should determine the services offered.[25]
The basic thrust of the release deals with a desire to promote
American carriers and protect them against foreign competition, with particular respect to the balance of payments.

Another source advances the opinion that bilateral agreements could be justified even if they obtained less for United
States carriers than they granted to foreign carriers "if for
example they succeeded in furthering international comity,
in promoting a free flow of men, goods, and ideas, and in
contributing to the solidarity of the western world."[26] These
would seem to be overwhelmingly important considerations.
Yet this writer's main thrust is that the bilateral route agreements entered into by the United States have in general been
too "generous," have resulted in an unreasonable drop in the
American carriers' share in international air transportation,
and illustrate what the author holds to be the excessive power
of the President to overrule the Civil Aeronautics Board and
make foreign policy considerations dominant over American
civil air transport interests.[27]

---

*One article suggests that in future years it will be con-
sidered astonishing that in the 1960's "reductions in trade barriers which would permit American consumers to obtain goods
and services at lower prices were referred to as 'concessions'
to other countries." Robert E. Asher, "U.N. Aid to the
U.S.," International Development, 2:15-9, June, 1965.

The one authority on civil aviation known to the present
writer who unequivocally gives primacy to the interests of the
world economy is the Netherlands writer, H. A. Wassenbergh,
who takes the flat position that the importance of the air
as a public highway should determine the law of the air and
outlaw the concept of bargainings for traffic rights based upon
reciprocity.[28]

POLITICAL CONSIDERATIONS

The political motives and objectives of governments in making
making civil aviation policy are numerous and varied and, to
some degree, take in virtually the entire spectrum of a government's political goals.

Deriving from the ultimate goal of preserving the existence
of the state are the military objectives such as the maintenance
of airports, airways, and civil flight crews, as well as commercial airline capacity for use by the military forces in an
emergency. In states with the capacity for aircraft manufacturing, the military interest calls for a strong manufacturing
base, as has been previously discussed.

A point of conflict between the political and the economic
should be mentioned here: Military leaders would like the
civil airline fleet to have the maximum possible excess (i.e.,
normally unutilized capacity in its regular operations. In
this way, should a national emergency arise, substantial air-
lift could be swiftly obtained with minimum disruption of the
regular airline services, which may be of increased importance
for the movement of executives, technicians, and cargo on
their regular runs. Clearly, though, the military advantage
conflicts with the economic disadvantage of overcapacity.

Previously discussed also were the psychological effects
of the spreading of airline networks from mother countries
to their colonies in the 1920's and 1930's. Airline routes have
also been established to areas where the airline's country
wishes to increase its political influence. A current example
would be the service of the Soviet airline from Moscow to
Havana.

There is a single, egregious example in aviation history
of the use of airlines as an instrument of political penetration:
the German penetration of Latin America in the 1930's by the
establishment of airlines (first with the Graf Zeppelin and
later with aircraft) from Germany via West Africa to Brazil,

and then the expansion of service across the South American continent. This program was noteworthy for several reasons: (1) It was a pioneering effort, often putting in airline service where none had ever existed, (2) Although beginning prior to the Nazi regime, it became an instrument of Nazi policy related to the concept of "Auslanddeutschtum," meaning the development of political ties between Germany and persons of German origin or descent, (3) German capital and technicians became deeply involved in the domestic airlines of South America, (4) All this became of heightened significance because of the Second World War.[29]

While such a net of circumstances could conceivably arise again, perhaps this time in Africa, the effectiveness of the penetration would be severely diluted by the fact that numerous airlines already crisscross even the relatively backward African continent. Political penetration through ownership or control of the airline of a new and backward nation is conceivable, although, with the strong spirit of anticolonialism pervading such countries today, it does not seem likely that such ownership or control would be welcomed or even permitted.

With the passing of most of the colonial empires, and with the great increase in the number of airlines and the amount of airline service throughout the world since the 1930's, the political objectives of colonial linkages and of political penetration of other areas would appear to have become factors of little practical significance in national aviation policies.

The more significant political objectives and motives today are those wherein a civil aviation action is traded against a non-aviation consideration. These can be quite specific "trades" as that which is believed to have occurred at the time of the United Kingdom-United States Bermuda Conference in 1946; the United Kingdom may have made concessions premised on its great need to obtain a substantial loan from the United States to meet postwar reconstruction needs.[30]

Less definite political exchanges are those where aviation is one factor in the promotion of good relations with another country in a general sense. Thus, it can be assumed that Iceland's membership in the North Atlantic Treaty Organization and its permitting American military bases on its territory, in the teeth of much domestic opposition, contribute to the continuing acquiescence of the United States in the operation by Icelandic Airlines of service between the United States and Europe at substantially lower fares than are charged by any other airline. (Another reason is that the Icelandic airline

uses "turboprop" rather than pure jet aircraft, thus offering
a substantially slower service. The airline does not belong
to the International Air Transport Association.) Similarly,
the Netherlands has obtained route grants which appear to have
been based in part on a general American policy of preserving
friendly relations with NATO members. [31]

Such political objectives are inherent in the process of
bargaining for bilateral route agreements, and would be absent under a multilateral agreement which did away with
route bargainings. It may seem at first glance that such bar-
gains would lead to economically unjustifiable air services;
but the opposite may occur, as when a government would like
to obstruct an economically justifiable foreign airline service
but refrains from doing so because it feels it to be of greater
importance to make what it construes as a "concession" to
please the foreign government in line with the larger political
relationship between the two countries.

To some degree the politics of the Cold War enters into
the picture. NATO policies have already been mentioned. In
the future, however, the political factor may be a tendency on
the part of both the United States and the Soviet Union to permit airlines of the new African republics to establish services
to the United States or the Soviet Union with no real justification
other than a prestige-seeking urge on the part of the small
country and a desire on the part of the large country to curry
favor or avoid offense. Developments, however, such as the
Air Afrique consortium described earlier, may ameliorate
this problem by creating economically viable airline services.

Another type of action related to Cold War politics in the
recent bilateral agreement between the United States and the
Soviet Union under which service between New York and Moscow by a Soviet and an American airline was instituted in
1968. The political motive here, far from being part of the
competitive effort between the two "superpowers," appears
to be a special case of the use of airline service as a friendly
gesture, intended to contribute to a lessening of the dangerous
tension between the two countries. Oddly enough, this agreement between two technologically advanced states resembles,
in its motivation, the practice in the early days of aviation
where an advanced country would extend its airline service to
a backward country as a deliberate gesture of friendship.

The highly political nature of the decision on each side to
establish the service is shown by the fact that, as a question
of good transportation between the two cities, the service was
largely superfluous, there having been New York-Moscow

airline service for over ten years by several Western European airlines such as the Belgian, Dutch, French, and Scandinavian. [32]

The Concept of World "Community"

It has been previously emphasized that a network of good
airline service is essential to the world economy. Similarly,
it appears that the world needs such a network in order to
facilitate and encourage the development of a world "community, " whether this latter term be construed as: (1) merely the
degree of good will among sovereign states that will minimize serious conflict, or (2) the degree of international cooperation which will enable the growth of the activities of the
United Nations and its specialized agencies, or (3) the premise, in a long-range sense, for some kind of larger world
polity.

Inis Claude, in taking issue with those advocates of world
government who have not properly measured the extraordinary
difficulties in the way of its achievement, speaks of "an or-
ganic, evolutionary conception of the slow growth of the
foundations of community feeling, the development of social
tissue, the enlargement of psychic and moral horizons, and
the emergence of common patterns of feeling and action. " [33]

Claude illustrates his point by quoting from another writer
to the effect that:

> All that is necessary to create the psychological
> foundation of a world society is that people in Maine
> should feel the same degree of responsibility toward
> the people of Japan or Chile or Indo-China as they
> feel toward California. That is pretty small, really,
> but it is apparently enough to create the United
> States. [34]

The contribution of transportation to the development of a
worldwide sense of community should be neither neglected
nor exaggerated. There seems little to quarrel with in the
statement made in a basic text in transportation that:

> Transportation makes for homogeneity of
> type, for the sympathy which comes from knowledge,
> and for the ease of cooperative action in non-
> economic as well as in economic matters which

comes from uniformity in customs, a common
point of view, and a likeness in environment. [35]

It should not, however, be uncritically assumed that an
improvement in a means of transport will automatically or
necessarily contribute to international cooperation. This
unquestioning assumption is made by Schenkman, who says:

> Air transport is particularly adapted to serve
> as a means of international intercourse, with the
> result that those deepened contacts bring about an
> increased spirit of international good will and dev-
> elop a feeling of brotherhood among the peoples of
> the world. . . .
> From the point of view of international rela-
> tions in the broadest sense, the more the peoples
> of the world are able to move around and see other
> ways of life, the more quickly shall we arrive at
> an age of peace and plenty. [36]

A sociologist, looking at the contribution of aviation to the
maintenance of the hold of a government over its people, uses
the expression esprit de corps rather than "community." Such
esprit de corps, he contends, can be built up from "frequency
of contacts," although he notes carefully that such contacts
do not necessarily lead to the desired rapport. He observes
that improved means of transportation have extended the possibilities for the establishment of larger communities. [37]
Another writer in a similar vein raises the question whether
aviation makes such larger communities a social necessity. [38]
The present writer would not hold that civil aviation, in
and of itself, makes larger political entities necessary, although it seems clearly to be one of a variety of technological
developments which make a higher degree of international
cooperation desirable for human welfare and conceivably even
for human survival.
Nor would he agree with Schenkman's assumption that
facilitating intercourse among peoples will automatically result in "peace and plenty." All an airline can do is move passengers, cargo, and mail; it cannot assure political wisdom.
It can bring diplomats swiftly to a conference table but cannot
determine what they will accomplish there. Indeed, increasing
the frequency of contacts between the peoples of two countries
could even, in some instance, promote conflicts which might
not have developed had they known little about each other.

The point to be emphasized, in conclusion, is that the interest of every nation in improving international cooperation and reducing international tensions ought to be an overriding consideration in foreign policy, which should carry over into that portion of foreign policy that deals with civil aviation. First, governments should beware of letting the bilateral system of route negotiations become a cause of ill will. But, more significantly, they should seek the growth of a network of efficient, low-cost airlines--apart from the question of the nationality of each--as a contribution toward the development of a world sense of community on which improved international cooperation can be built. Governments should resist the habit of neglecting this broad general political objective which they all share, should resist the habit of concentrating on more immediate, but in the long run far less weighty, considerations.

NOTES

1. Oliver J. Lissitzyn, International Air Transport and National Policy (New York: Council on Foreign Relations, 1942), pp. 14 and 58.

2. Michel Pourcelet, "The International Element in Air Transportation," Journal of Air Law and Commerce, 33:78, 1967.

3. United States Civil Aeronautics Board Orders E-24596 and E-24597, January 4, 1967.

4. Lissitzyn, op. cit., pp. 5-9; Jacob Schenkman, International Civil Aviation Organization (Geneva: Librairie E. Droz, 1955), p. 20.

5. Stuart Daggett, Principles of Inland Transportation (Third edition; New York: Harper and Brothers, 1941), p. 22.

6. Handbook of Airline Statistics (Washington: Government Printing Office, 1967), p. 23; United Nations Statistical Yearbook (New York: United Nations, 1967), p. 549.

7. Air Transport World, (February, 1969), pp. 21-4.

8. Myres S. McDougal, Harold D. Lasswell, and Ivan A. Vlasic, Law and Public Order in Space (New Haven: Yale University Press, 1963), p. 250.

9. Robert A. Nelson, "Scandinavian Airlines System: A Case of International Cooperation" (unpublished doctoral dissertation, Clark University, Worcester, 1954), p. 29.

10. Nelson, op. cit., p. 188.

11. Air Transport World, (October, 1968), pp. 50-2.

12. Edwin T. Haefele, "Transport Planning and National Goals," Transport and National Goals (Washington: The Brookings Institution, 1969), pp. 184-5.

13. Raul Prebisch, "Commercial Policy in the Underdeveloped Countries," American Economic Review, 49:251-73, (May, 1959); A. K. Das-Gupta, Planning and Economic Growth (London: George Allen and Unwin, 1965), pp. 136-7.

14. Raul Prebisch, Towards a New Trade Policy For Development (New York: United Nations, 1964), p. 59.

15. Frederick C. Thayer, Jr., Air Transport Policy and National Security (Chapel Hill: University of North Carolina Press, 1965), p. 284.

16. Aviation Week and Space Technology, (March 10, 1969), pp. 179-84.

17. Air Transport World, (February, 1969), pp. 21-4.

18. Ibid., (January, 1969), p. 29.

19. Official Airline Guide, (February, 1969). See also news item concerning Aeroflot in Soviet Life, (August, 1967), p. 39, which states that "most of the flying is domestic."

20. For a discussion of this general question, see Cooper, The Right To Fly, op. cit., and, for a more modern treatment, Thayer, Air Transport Policy and National Security, op. cit.

21. Hugh G. Smith, "Shannon Salute," New York Times, September 6, 1964, Section X, p. 15.

22. Norman Macras, "No Christ on the Andes," The Economist, October 1, 1965, unnumbered special insert section.

23. H. Max Healey, "Revisions to the Mexico-United States Air Transport Agreement, 1965-1970," Journal of Air Law and Commerce, 32:175, 1966.

24. As is done in Charles M. Sackrey, Jr., "Overcapacity in the United States International Air Transport Industry," Journal of Air Law and Commerce, 32:24-93, 1966.

25. Statement on International Air Transport Policy, A Report prepared by an Interagency Steering Committee (Washington: The White House, 1963), p. 8.

26. Eugene A. Weibel, "International Civil Aviation and Federal Power" (unpublished Doctoral dissertation, Harvard University, 1962), p. 516.

27. Ibid., pp. 12 and 517-20.

28. H. A. Wassenbergh, Post-War International Civil Aviation Policy and the Law of the Air (The Hague: Martinus Nijhoff, 1962), pp. 137-41 and 157.

29. For an excellent discussion of the German penetration of South America, see Lissitzyn, op. cit., pp. 315-58.

30. Henry Ladd Smith, Airways Abroad (Madison: University of Wisconsin Press, 1950), p. 256.

31. Oliver J. Lissitzyn, "Bilateral Agreements on Air Transport," Journal of Air Law and Commerce, 30:254, 1964.

32. Hans Haymann, Jr., "The Soviet Role in Civil Aviation," Journal of Air Law and Commerce, 25:265-80, 1958.

33. Inis L. Claude, Jr., Swords Into Plowshares (third edition; New York: Random House, 1964), p. 378.

34. Ibid., p. 379, citing Kenneth Boulding in Quincy Wright (ed.), The World Community (Chicago: University of Chicago Press, 1948), pp. 101-2.

35. Stuart Daggett, Principles of Inland Transportation, op. cit., p. 22.

36. Jacob Schenkman, International Civil Aviation Organization (Geneva: Librairie E. Droz, 1955), pp. 5-6.

37. William Fielding Ogburn, The Social Effects of Aviation (Boston: Houghton Mifflin Co., 1946), pp. 695-6.

38. D. Goedhuis, Idea and Interest in International Aviation (The Hague: Martinus Nijhoff, 1947), p. 8.

5

THE
COMPETITIVE SITUATION
OF WORLD AIRLINE SERVICES

OLIGOPOLY: THE PREVAILING SYSTEM

The term "oligopoly" appears to be the appropriate one
to describe the market situation with respect to world airline
service, just as it applies to the United States domestic sys-
tem--i.e., service is offered in each market by a limited
number of suppliers.

The limitations in both cases, however, derive from
political rather than economic forces. Within the American
domestic system, the maximum number of carriers in each
market is controlled by the certification requirement, while
the minimum number is maintained by such devices as merger
controls and protective rate regulation. In the world system,
the maximum number in a market is controlled through bilateral negotiations, while the minimum number is maintained
by capacity and rate controls which prevent the weaker airlines from being overwhelmed by the stronger.

The number, however, in the world system tends to be
greater than in the American domestic system in generally
comparable city pairs--e.g., seven airlines between New
York and Paris, three between New York and San Francisco.
The discrepancy is greater if the basis for comparison is the
general market between broad areas--e.g., twenty-three
between the United States and Europe, seven between the East
Coast and West Coast of the United States. [1] (It should be kept
in mind that traffic between points in the same country is reserved as "cabotage" to the airlines of that country, as a
virtually universal principle.)

116

Since the world system is premised on route exchanges negotiated among sovereign states, it is not surprising that the number of airlines between broad areas is related to the number of states in each area. All but the tiniest countries of Western Europe, and all but three of the states of Central and South America, now have airlines serving the United States. In the Pacific area, the number of states is smaller and the number of airlines less; there are, for example, seven (plus one all-cargo line) between the United States and the Far East. [2]

Only with respect to Africa is it not true that numerous states breed numerous airlines. The reasons are the newness, smallness, and economic and technological backwardness of most of the states, the lean traffic with the rest of the world, and their location away from the heavily traveled world air routes.

Although the bilateral system has not prevented even some relatively small countries from establishing long-range world airline services, the political barriers which an airline must hurdle (both of its own and foreign governments) in order to establish an international service effectively limit the number of carriers to a degree consistent with the designation "oligopoly." Furthermore, the competitive behavior of the airlines reveals many of the characteristics associated with any industry with a limited number of suppliers--e. g., competition is extreme with respect to relatively minor aspects of the service offered, whereas there is highly controlled price competition.

One writer, Frederick C. Thayer, Jr., compares the airlines to the petroleum industry in the United States with its wastefully prolific retail gasoline service stations and massive advertising to the retail market. He compares these practices to the airline practices "of nonrational capacity and the use of advertising on an extremely large scale." [3]

Another writer, Richard E. Caves, states that: "The high levels of fares (maintained by cartel agreements) in international travel, coupled with the national-prestige motives influencing most foreign carriers, moan that product and quality competition is even more fierce there than in the American domestic market." [4]

The present writer would condition the last statement by noting that the largely undifferentiated product involved narrows the possibilities for "product and quality competition" so that the emphasis is on minor amenities such as meals, liquor service, and in-flight moving pictures. In fact, in a study of the North Atlantic market, the conclusion is reached that the

IATA carriers ". . . have created a market with almost no price competition and where other aspects of competition are very restricted. "[5] Perhaps the one important gain to the consumer from service competition is greater frequency of service, including more nonstop services.

The pricing situation reminds one of the "administered prices" of the large industrial oligopolies of the United States, except that the "price fixing" in the case of IATA is done openly at airline conferences and with governmental approvals. (Formal approval in the United States by the Civil Aeronautics Board legally relieves the American carriers of antitrust law violations.)*

IS MONOPOLY POSSIBLE OR DESIRABLE IN INTERNATIONAL AIRLINE SERVICE?

It can be argued that airline service, if left wholly without political or economic regulation, would ultimately result in a single monopoly carrier between each pair of cities. There has never been any demonstration of such an event and there is not likely to be any since governments would never permit it to occur.

Monopoly established by government fiat, however, is quite another matter. It now exists within many domestic spheres, where a government permits only one airline, often a government-owned corporation, to operate all domestic services. It also exists in the United States where service to many small cities is limited to a single, subsidized "local service air carrier. "

For a monopoly situation to exist in an international market, however, it would appear necessary to have a world airline such as that proposed at Chicago in 1944 by Australia and New Zealand, or at least regional airlines operated jointly by the governments of each region, using the latter term to

---

*Where agreement cannot be reached at airline conferences, however, or where governments veto such agreements, an "open rate" situation may occur. In such cases, the airlines usually continue existing rates pending working out of the problem, but they are free to charge any rate they select (subject to approval of governments of the countries on each route.) The IATA system thus can turn quickly from tight control to chaotic price-cutting.

mean, for example: (1) both sides of the Atlantic with respect to transatlantic service, (2) both sides of the Pacific with respect to transpacific service, and (3) the whole Western Hemisphere with respect to flights between the United States and Latin America.

It seems impractical to suggest that such international operating agencies might be established in the current world political climate. Even where a substantial sense of community exists on a political level--as between the United States and Western Europe--it seems scarcely credible that a regional carrier operating all North Atlantic air services as one vast monopoly would be acceptable.

Even if acceptable politically, however, an international monopoly operation is of questionable desirability, saving the limited case where traffic in a market is so thin that only one carrier can be supported. A monopoly would place the consumers of the world or region at the mercy of one entity, albeit an international one. The downright arrogance often associated with a monopoly need not necessarily be absent simply because the monopoly is the creature of a number of governments or of an international authority.

A monopoly carrier might be laggard in the purchase of the newest, fastest, and most comfortable aircraft. The opposite, however, might occur: a rational balance might be struck between discarding too soon the older aircraft and delaying too long in acquiring the new. It might be easier to strike such a balance from a monopoly position than in a fiercely competitive market. Much would seem to depend on the nature of the management and of the international governmental regulation of the monopoly. Similarly, with the cost of air service, monopoly could bode either good or ill for the consumer, depending on management and the effectiveness of international regulation.

A conceivable use of a monopoly carrier, though one of limited applicability, would involve service by the national airline of country A between a point in country A and a point in country B, by prior agreement of the governments of both countries. The national airline of country B would then have a comparable monopoly between a different pair of points in the two countries. The likelihood of such an arrangement, however, seems limited to neighboring countries where relatively small cities are involved. The need to exclude all third countries from the traffic would, of course, involve a denial of Fifth Freedom rights.

As a practical matter, then, monopoly situations in world airline markets are highly unlikely to occur.

IS UNREGULATED COMPETITION POSSIBLE OR
DESIRABLE IN INTERNATIONAL AIRLINE SERVICE?

A number of authorities have questioned the need for
regulation of the domestic trunklines of the United States, and
have implied that removal of all or most of such regulation
would be helpful rather than harmful to the public. While such
an experiment within the United States would be possible if
authorized by Congress, it seems inconceivable that it could
be tried in the international domain since the whole history of
air transportation demonstrates that governments are not prepared to throw their national carriers to the mercies of the
marketplace. Nor is it likely that governments would accept
the idea that an economic function so vital to the public welfare
should be thrown to the determinations of the marketplace.
However, although unregulated competition (which, of
course, would mean tearing up the bilateral agreements, the
IATA rate machinery, and all limitations whatever on entry
and capacity) can be dismissed as politically impractical, the
argument that, as a matter of pure economics, airline competition need not be regulated at all (or very little) will be examined here since it has a bearing on the question of what
degree and kind of regulation should be accepted for the world's
airlines. If the argument is correct, then it might fairly be
concluded that the regulation of competition imposed in the
current system--i. e., by the bilateral agreements, the Bermuda and other capacity controls, and the IATA and governmental rate controls--is merely a concession to the world
political system and is hurtful from an economic standpoint.
In an early study by Frederick W. Gill and Gilbert L.
Bates, measuring the competitive situation in certain major
American markets, the conclusion was advanced that there
should be no more than two airlines serving between any pair
of cities. Two was the ideal number because the evils of
monopoly were removed--the passenger had a choice and the
airline a motive for pleasing him; but the diseconomics from
wasteful advertising and duplication of facilities were mini-
mized. [6]
This concept is assailed by both Caves and Thayer who
contend that the study of Gill and Bates was far too narrow.
For example, that study covered a period before, during, and
immediately after World War II, and may not be pertinent to
a less disturbed time. Also, it covered events only through
1948, measuring in particular what were immediate, rather

than long-run, effects of the addition of third carriers to
various markets in the 1946-47 period.

Thayer favors regulated monopoly. He finds two airlines
in a market to be one too many and to offer all the wasteful
practices that would exist if there were more than two. [7]

Caves holds that it is difficult to estimate the maximum
number of airlines that can serve between two points without
a rising average cost. He states that "the only workable
approach seems to be the behavioral one of looking at the number of carriers actually operating in various sizes of city-pair
markets."[8] He advocates two or three in any one transcon-
tinental market, and four or five in short or medium hauls,
and predicts that these numbers are not likely to rise because
future growth of traffic will be accompanied by even greater
growth in the amount of traffic necessary for a carrier to
break even, due to the use of larger, more expensive aircraft.
He advocates, however, not a designation by governmental
authority of the correct number of airlines to serve between
each city pair, but instead an opening of entry to major city
pairs to the existing trunklines and, subsequently, to any airline, including a completely new business entity.

Caves argues that destructive competition would not result
because the trunklines have fleets of established size and a
"recognized mutual dependence," and these factors would prevent any great overinvestment of capital in new aircraft. Route
structures, he contends, would come closer to balance, and
seasonal utilization of aircraft would improve. There would
be mergers and a rationalizing of the networks of the trunklines, and rate controls could then be taken off so that the
Civil Aeronautics Board, with respect to the domestic trunklines, would be no more than a promotional agency and not a
regulatory one at all. (Services to minor points, offered by
the local-service air carriers, would continue to be regulated
and subsidized.)[9]

Another writer, Dudley F. Pegrum, while not specifically
saying that all regulation should be removed from the American
domestic trunklines, appears to favor at least a great reduction in such regulation. He seems to be concluding that in the
absence of evidence that airline service is a "natural monopoly"
(such as railroads and pipelines), it is naturally "competitive."[10] (This position would appear to neglect the whole
field of the imperfect and indeed sometimes minimal competition of the oligopoly.)

Pegrum holds that public policy in regulating transport
industries should be based on "the competitive model" rather

than "the model for monopoly or any variation of it, " because
the latter "lacks standards by which to gauge the economical
allocation of resources. "[11] He holds also that restriction on
the number of airlines is probably not necessary, that minimum rate control is necessary only where subsidy is being
paid, and that maximum rate control is an indication that
additional competition should be permitted. [12]

Still another writer, Lucille Keyes, dwelling on the
question of freedom of entry into the American domestic trunk-
line system, suggests that perhaps controls on entry should
be removed, but that competition should continue to be regulated through broad use of the present powers of the Civil
Aeronautics Board to approve or disapprove inter-carrier
agreements such as those dividing markets, restricting rates,
or restricting the introduction of service innovations. Rates
would be regulated only "to prevent deliberate elimination or
exclusion of competition by temporary below-cost rate cutting. "[13]

The concept that airlines can be left as unregulated as
such major American industries as automobiles, steel, and
electronics appears based, first, on an assumption that it is
desirable to leave the latter oligopolies as little regulated as
they are--i. e. , subject only to antitrust laws--and, second,
on an assumption that there is no distinction to be drawn between such industries and the common-carrier transportation
services of the nation. The automobile and steel industries
have a single company that is a price "leader, " and price
increases in either of these industries (and perhaps other
major industries such as electronics) can shake the whole
economy to a degree where, an overwhelming case exists, in
the public interest, for a type of federal regulation, generally
similar to that imposed historically on the common carriers.
In short, airlines should not be permitted to follow the socially
irresponsible pattern of the great American industrial oligopolies.

Should one disagree with this opinion, however, there
remains the consideration that common-carrier transportation
possesses a crucial social and economic value of a degree and
kind setting it beyond such industries as steel and automobiles
in terms of a need for public control. In the economy, and as
a social service to the public, it is as vital as the postal and
telephone services.

Let it be assumed for the moment, purely for the sake of
argument, that removal of economic regulation from American
domestic trunklines, or from the world's airlines, would

result in balanced competition among equally low-cost and efficient carriers. Even in such an ideal competitive situation, the public would need protection in ways where the profit motive either would not impel the carriers to act in the public interest or would impel to them to act contrary to it.

Thus, service to less profitable points may be curtailed as each airline seeks the optimum use of its capital. Serious undercapacity for peak days and peak seasons might develop if the airlines saw their private economic interest in seeking the highest possible average annual load factor. Discrimination in favor of a client (such as a major shipper or a firm with substantial business travel) or to a class of customer or to a locality might well occur. These matters all involve judgments as to what is a "reasonable" construction of the public's right to certain services, or a "reasonable" balance between conflicting interests. Common carrier law in the United States places many of these judgments in the hands of a regulatory body--i. e. , a public authority--which may require a carrier to act contrary to its private profit-motivated interest.

In effect, the body of common-carrier law which has developed in the United States is based on the premise that public scheduled transportation is an industry particularly and peculiarly affected with the public interest to a degree where the public has certain rights transcending the profit motive of the carriers. A similar philosophy is implied in the prevalent practice of other countries of making the national air carrier a public corporation.

The conclusion, then, concerning the regulation of competition is that it is not only (for the world system) politically unavoidable, but is highly desirable from the standpoint of the public welfare.

REGULATED COMPETITION

Not only is regulated competition the prevalent system in world airline service, and the inevitable one from the political standpoint in the foreseeable future, but it is the most desirable system from the standpoint of world public interest.

That regulated competition is the preferable system was asserted by Lissitzyn in 1942 and by the Netherlands writer Goedhuis in 1952, the latter using the term "ordered competition."[14] Wheatcroft concludes that ". . . unregulated competition leads to excessive capacity, disorderly market

conditions, financial instability of the carriers and consequently
undependable service to the public, " although he notes that this
conclusion may be diluted with respect to busy city pairs in
future years "if the scale of the market becomes sufficiently
large to permit free multi-carrier competition. " He praises
the United States system of domestic airline regulation as
"the most comprehensive and satisfactory system. "[15]

Another writer, Samuel B. Richmond, after a study of the
American domestic system, concludes: "What is clear is
that some blend is superior to the exclusive use of one or the
other mechanism; i. e. , a single monopoly carrier for the
nation, or alternatively, unrestricted competition . . . . The
optimum blend of competition and regulation is a dynamic
quantity. "[16]

Of some pertinence at this point, though not specifically
referring to aviation, is a statement by Senator J. William
Fulbright:

> We can neither abolish nor totally accept national
> rivalries; we have got, somehow, to put them under
> some restraints, just as we have brought the rival-
> ries of business and other groups within our own
> society under restraints in order to protect the com-
> munity and, indeed, in order to perpetuate competi-
> tion, which under conditions of unregulated rivalry
> would soon enough be ended with the elimination of
> the small and weak groups by the big and strong
> ones. [17]

The question to be considered, then, is whether, granted
the desirability and inevitability of regulated competition, the
present world system of regulation is the best one or whether
increased international control should be favored as, for
example, the system proposed by Canada at the crucial point
of the Chicago Conference, or those proposed in the 1946
Draft or 1947 Draft. The current system offers the immediate
objection that no central planning is possible since regulation
is by different governments at different times pursuing varying
policies toward different aspects of airline service. The
proverb about too many cooks spoiling the broth suggests itself.

NOTES

1. Official Airline Guide, (April, 1969).

2. Ibid., (January, 1970).

3. Frederick C. Thayer, Jr., Air Transport Policy and National Security (Chapel Hill: University of North Carolina Press, 1965), pp. 289-90.

4. Richard E. Caves, Air Transport and its Regulators (Cambridge: Harvard University Press, 1962), p. 307.

5. Harold K. Strom, "The North Atlantic Air Transport Market--A Study of the American Competitive Position" (unpublished Doctoral dissertation, University of California at Los Angeles, 1964), p. xvii.

6. Frederick W. Gill and Gilbert L. Bates, Airline Competition (Boston: Harvard University Press, 1949).

7. Thayer, op. cit., pp. 296-7.

8. Caves, op. cit., pp. 95-6.

9. Caves, op. cit., pp. 433 and 447-8.

10. Dudley F. Pegrum, Transportation: Economics and Public Policy (Homewood, Illinois: Richard D. Irwin, Inc., 1963), pp. 139-40, 373-4, and 426.

11. Ibid., p. 157.

12. Ibid., p. 188.

13. Lucille Keyes, Federal Control of Entry Into Air Transportation (Cambridge: Harvard University Press, 1951), pp. 340-6.

14. Lissitzyn, op. cit., pp. 250 and 276-7; D. Goedhuis, "Questions of Public International Air Law," Recueil des Cours, 81:294, 1952.

15. Wheatcroft, op. cit., p. 214.

16. Samuel B. Richmond, <u>Regulation and Competition in Air Transportation</u> (New York: Columbia University Press, 1961), p. 257.

17. J. William Fulbright, <u>The Arrogance of Power</u> (New York: Random House, 1966), p. 162.

6

It remains, then, to draw some conclusions from the foregoing survey of objectives, problems, and attempts at international governance.

The complexity of the problems, and of the larger question of how to resolve them, will by now be evident. The conclusions to be drawn, accordingly, will be suggestive rather than dogmatic. They will be divided as follows: (1) an attempt to select the best of the several systems analyzed earlier in this study, and (2) an attempt to delineate desirable changes in the philosophy of peoples and governments toward the international economic regulation of airlines. The point will be emphasized that the system to be adopted is only a mechanism, and that it is the peoples and governments who must, so to speak, operate the machine. Thus, even under the present system, with its minimal formal international machinery, a considerable improvement in the working of the system could be achieved merely by a change in philosophy.

The first question--what is the best system?--will be considered in three parts: (1) a brief summary of the present system and of the major proposals for varying degrees of multilateralism; (2) the best one of these systems, having regard to world, rather than a national, public interest; and (3) a "second-best" system which, perhaps, should be sought now as more likely to be obtained than the first choice.

WHAT IS THE BEST SYSTEM?

A Review of Main Points in the Several Systems

Table 2 attempts to break down, in a highly simplified
form, the major provisions of the present and each proposed
system--the Canadian compromise proposed at Chicago, the
1946 Draft, the 1947 Majority Draft, the Minority Draft of the
same year, and the Geneva Draft. (Pertinent provisions of
the latter four drafts appear as Appendixes B-E.)
Although the table is largely self-explanatory, a few
salient points might be emphasized. Under "Routes," the
Canadian Chicago compromise Draft,* the 1946 Draft, and
the 1947 Majority Draft all would abolish the system of bilateral negotiations--i.e., in effect, would remove the implicit embargo on the establishment of airline services around
which every government must negotiate--and would permit
the unilateral establishment of airline service to any country
by any airline, subject, of course, to various limitations as
briefly noted in the table.
The 1947 Minority Draft, however, and the Geneva Draft,
would continue the bilateral system, although the former would
include a clause to the effect that a route should not be refused
for any reason other than an "insufficiency of traffic."
Under "Frequency and Capacity," the Canadian Draft is
unique in that it would not adopt the Bermuda language wherein
capacity and frequency are subject only to ex post facto controls under certain general principles. Instead, it would use
a predetermination of capacity in accordance with a rather
elaborate formula involving "sectors," "divisions," and an
escalator, as described in Chapter 2. (The Canadian proposal
was, of course, made in 1944, prior to the Bermuda Conference.) All other systems would involve the Bermuda approach.
Similarly, with respect to Fifth Freedom, the Canadian
Draft is unique in that it employs a formula for predetermining
the amount of capacity that can be justified on the basis of a
presumed carriage of Fifth Freedom traffic. However, there
is a resemblance between the Canadian and Bermuda Fifth

---

*This will be referred to herein, for brevity's sake,
simply as the "Canadian Draft," although it was not the original Canadian proposal at Chicago but merely the ultimate offer of Canada in an effort to bring the American and British
positions together.

TABLE 2

Major Provisions of Systems of International Economic Regulation of Airlines

	Present System	Canadian Draft	1946 Draft	1947 Draft (Majority)	1947 Draft (Minority)	Geneva Draft
Routes	Bilateral	Unilateral to/from home country	Unilateral to/from home country	Unilateral on four months notice	Bilateral, but may decline only for insufficiency of traffic	Bilateral
Frequency/capacity	Bermuda, but some with pre-determination	Formula*	Bermuda, but with international body overseeing	Bermuda	Bermuda	Bermuda
Fifth Freedom	Bermuda, but some stricter	Assume Fifth will equal half of Third in justifying capacity	Bermuda, but rate differential may be used	Bermuda	Bermuda	Bermuda
Rates	Airline conferences and governments	Airline conferences and govts., but ICAO Council, on appeal, may "recommend" rates	Airline conferences and govts., but ICATB, on appeal, may prescribe rates	Airline conferences and governments	Airline conferences and governments	Airline conferences and governments
Internat'l regulatory body	None	None, but ICAO Council assigns capacity by prescribed formulas	ICATB, with true regulatory powers	None	None	None

* Canadian formula: initial capacity of 50 percent Third Freedom level (minimum one flight a week); escalator thereafter, using concept of sectors and divisions.

Freedom provisions in that the Canadians did not envisage
the predetermination of precise quantities of Fifth Freedom
traffic that could be carried, but would have permitted the
filling of any empty seats with such traffic subject only to
language making Fifth Freedom a weaker justification than
Third/Fourth for a capacity increase.

Under the heading "Rates" in the table, there appears a
surprising similarity among the systems. Both the current
and all proposed systems involve agreed rates, negotiated
among airlines, airline conferences, and governments. The
one significant difference is that in the 1946 Draft, in the absence of agreement after prolonged negotiations, it would be
possible for a party to appeal to an international regulatory
body which, after hearings, could prescribe a rate.

An international regulatory body would not even exist
under any of the other systems, except the Canadian in the
sense that the latter gave the ICAO Council certain powers to
recommend rates on appeal.

All of the systems provide for some form of third party
settlement of disputes, whether through the ICAO Council, an
arbitral tribunal, or the International Court of Justice.[*] Also,
all systems provide for denunciation of the multilateral agreement on one year's notice. The significance of the latter is
that were one of the multilateral systems to be tried and
found extremely injurious by a state, it could use its power
of denunciation to serve notice forcefully on all other parties
of its extreme displeasure with the way the new system was
working out. Very likely it would obtain some degree of re-
lief or some measure of accommodation prior to the end of
the one-year period, enabling it to withdraw its notice. Failing this, however, it would have the ultimate power to simply
step out of the whole multilateral arrangement.

---

[*]Note, however, that although many bilateral agreements (twenty-one out of fifty-five in the case of the United
States as of 1965) provide for requesting the ICAO Council
for an advisory opinion in case of a dispute, no such use of
the Council has ever been made. Furthermore, there is
doubt whether the Council can perform such a service since
the basic Chicago Convention gives it no such function. See
Oliver J. Lissitzyn, "International Aspects of Air Transport
in American Law," Journal of Air Law and Commerce, 33:96-7.

The Best of the Various Systems

The best system from the standpoint of world public interest is, in the opinion of the present writer, the 1946 Draft. In developing this conclusion, use will be made of Table 3, wherein an attempt is made to evaluate the present and proposed systems as "good," "fair," or "poor," with respect to certain specified objectives--i.e., simplification, centralized economic planning, lower fares, the welfare of the less developed countries (LDCs), and the general contribution to world peace.

Simplification

The simplification of the present maze of bilateral agreements, with their varying provisions on such basic matters as capacity and Fifth Freedom, can best be achieved by those proposals which would scrap the bilateral system in favor of a multilateral exchange of the right to establish routes. Thus, the Canadian, the 1946, and the 1947 Majority Drafts are rated "good," although it is noted that the Canadian would introduce a complexity of its own in the formula approach with its "sector" and "escalator" provisions. The 1947 Minority and Geneva Drafts would retain the bilateral system but would introduce a uniformity of rules with respect to capacity and Fifth Freedom; thus, they would make at least some contribution to simplification, and are rated "fair." The present system must necessarily be rated "poor."

Centralized Economic Planning

While both the present and all the proposed systems will leave the world airlines in a state of regulated competition (believed by the present writer to be both inevitable and desirable), the regulation in the absence of a central body is necessarily a responsibility scattered among the various governments and applied variously and inconsistently through such matters as bilateral route negotiations, amendments to existing bilateral agreements, capacity consultations, and the elaborate rate bargainings of the IATA machinery.

Those systems lacking a central regulatory body must thus be rated "poor," which means that only the Canadian and 1946 Drafts can be given a rating of "good." Of the two, however, the 1946 Draft offers a central body with more extensive powers than does the Canadian.

TABLE 3

Evaluation of Present and Proposed Systems of Airline Regulation*

Objective	Present System	Canadian Draft (1944)	1946 Draft	1947 Draft (Majority)	1947 Draft (Minority)	Geneva Draft (1947)
Simplification	Poor	Good	Good	Good	Fair	Fair
Centralized economic planning	Poor	Good	Good	Poor	Poor	Poor
Lower fares	Fair	Fair	Good	Fair	Fair	Fair
Welfare of the LDCs	Poor	Good	Good	Fair	Poor	Fair
Contribution to world peace	Poor	Good	Good	Fair	Poor	Poor

* The systems are assessed from the standpoint of a general world public interest (as outlined in Chapter 4) rather than the interest of any one nation. These are, of necessity, the subjective estimates of the writer.

It may be questioned whether the rather elaborate and intricate problems of regulating a public utility which, in American practice, are handled by the peculiar political institution, a "Public Utilities Commission," can be effectively carried out by a similar agency on an international level. Presumably, the International Civil Air Transport Board (to be abbreviated herein as ICATB) conceived by the 1946 Draft would include representatives of different political and cultural traditions. It would unquestionably face difficulties in working out both procedural and substantive problems by the very reason of the newness to international administration of a body of this sort. It would certainly not be easy for men of differing traditions, coming from nations with perhaps quite different economic backgrounds and problems, to operate in the rather curious manner that is demanded of an economic regulatory agency wherein a member must be both an impartial "expert" and something of a politician as well, and where he must operate in a medium that combines and blurs the executive, legislative, and judicial functions.

There seems no reason, however, to despair of the possibility of such an agency functioning effectively. For one thing, the 1946 Draft limits the burden that would be placed on it. It would not have to determine every question of capacity or Fifth Freedom; instead, day-to-day problems along these lines would be worked out by the airlines and governments under the Bermuda principles, with the ICATB merely in the background to deal with disputes which could not otherwise be resolved. Similarly, the Draft places the rate-making function upon the ICATB on an appellate basis only, so that only the occasional difficult case would fall to it to resolve.

There is, furthermore, no reason to assume that a higher level of government is less efficient than a lower; whether this is the case depends on the particular problem of government involved. Just as such functions as fire protection and garbage disposal are best handled by a city administration, whereas interstate commerce within the United States is best handled on a federal level, so such a matter as international air travel, which is by its nature patently international, may well be most efficiently governed at an international level.[1]

Lower Fares

As has been earlier stated, the great disappointment of international airline service with respect to the world public interest has been that the astonishing gains in the speed of travel have not been accompanied by equally astonishing gains with respect to lowered fares.

An example of this is that, at the present writing (mid-1969), it is possible to charter a large jet aircraft for a round trip between New York and London at a cost of about $150 as the prorated share of each person on board. This figure assumes that every seat is occupied--i.e., that the load factor is 100 percent, as may well occur on a chartered flight when an organization plans long in advance to conduct the flight and is at pains to see that the plane is sold out to its membership. Since a scheduled service can be expected to operate with a year-round load factor of only about 50 percent, it is necessary to double the $150 to arrive at a reasonable estimate of a fare for a scheduled New York-London round-trip flight, or $300. Yet the minimum regular fare between these points, as agreed upon by the IATA airlines and their governments, is $420 in the off season and $510 in the summer months.

Thus, it can be concluded that the fare in the previous example is about 50 percent higher than it should be or, put another way, that it should be reduced by one third.*

On this important objective, however, the mechanism by which fares are arrived at appears of less significance than the philosophies under which airlines and governments approach the various negotiations through the IATA system. The present system could achieve substantial reductions in fares if the airlines and governments were to decide to use the system to that end.

---

* There are, to be sure, a variety of special fares which permit some persons to obtain transatlantic scheduled service at fares considerably lower than the "Economy Class" shown above. By purchasing an inclusive tour lasting at least two and not over three weeks, one may obtain a fare of $230 New York-London round trip (not counting the cost of the land tour). Without purchase of a tour, one may obtain an "excursion" fare ranging between $300 and $410 (depending on season and day of the week), but the return trip must be made in not less than two or more than three weeks. These curious fares are designed to capture segments of the tourist market which would not, for the most part, travel at the higher "Economy Class" fares. For purposes of this study, however, it cannot be accepted that the world public interest is being well served by fares directed to persons whose plans lend themselves to round-trip travel within specified time periods.

IATA can readily be blamed for giving the world high fares since it is the mechanism through which the higher-cost carriers, using the unanimity rule of IATA conferences, prevent adequate fare reductions, and through which certain airlines seek to derive profits from their transatlantic services to cover losses from services to less heavily traveled areas. However, it is submitted that the villain in the piece is not the IATA mechanism but rather the combination of two facts: (1) that the economic characteristics of airline service virtually compel the charging of the same fares by all the airlines in one market, and (2) that the political division of the world into sovereign states gives each government a veto over the fares to be charged by all airlines serving its territory. IATA, then, is only a mechanism reflecting a combination of the economic fact with the political fact.

The present system, considered just as a mechanism, is rated "fair" with respect to lower fares, as are all the other proposed systems except the 1946 Draft. The reasoning is that the two 1947 and the Geneva Drafts would simply retain the current system with respect to international rate making, while the Canadian Draft would retain the current system with an international regulatory body with unclear, but presumably only advisory powers on disputed rate questions. (The Canadian Draft, hammered out under pressure at the Chicago Conference, appears to have concentrated on capacity and Fifth Freedom problems rather than rate problems.)

Only the 1946 Draft offers hope of international rate making where the mechanism will be an improvement; it would retain the complete IATA system but would set above it a regulatory body which, on appeal, could hold hearings concerning rates and actually prescribe what it deemed reasonable fares.

No one, of course, can safely predict what impact on international fares such an appeals system might have. More than likely, the basic rate making would still be carried out largely by airline conferences, supervised by governments, as today. But the knowledge that a body of experts with responsibility on an international plane rather than to national governments might forcefully represent the world's consumers, should an appeal come before them, could well have a salutary effect on the airline conferences and governments, even if very few rate actions were appealed.

There can, of course, be no assurance that the members of such a body would take this world view. Yet the Board was to have consisted of men elected by the Assembly of ICAO

and paid salaries by ICAO itself at levels to be determined by
the Assembly. While their accountability to the Assembly,
rather than to their own governments, is thus clear, their
selection could well reflect the prevailing philosophies of the
Assembly members, who are, of course, instructed representatives of their governments. A political compromise in
the election of ICATB members could result in representation
of various philosophies--e.g., one man known to attach primary emphasis to lowering fares, another tending to place
primary weight on protecting airlines from financial losses
by a conservative approach to the fare structure.

The term of office was not decided in the 1946 Draft, it
being specified only that there would be from five to seven
members, the exact number as well as the term of office to
be determined by the Assembly. Should such a Board ever
be established, it can at least be hoped that the Assembly
would follow the experience of the United States Government
with its regulatory agencies and provide for terms of office
of substantial length (e.g., six or seven years). A member
with such tenure would be encouraged to identify with a general world public interest, apart from or even contrary to the
interests of his own government or its airlines.

Thus, the 1946 Draft offers a substantial hope that lower
fares could better be achieved under this mechanism than
under the present system or any of the other proposals. But
the central point remains that the will to work for such fares
must become more widespread among member governments
if there is to be progress.

At this writing, it appears likely that within a year the
so-called jumbo jet aircraft, seating as many as 500 passengers
(at maximum seating density), will enter the market.* Although such mass production of airline service will permit
great cost savings (for example, crew expense per passenger),
it is being argued by some airlines and governments that there
can be no fare reduction whatever when these aircraft are
introduced. And, in fact, the argument is even being heard
that an increase in fares may be necessary to compensate
the airlines for losses they fear from empty seats on under-
utilized aircraft.**

_____

*Since preparation of the above, one type of jumbo jet
aircraft, the Boeing 747, has been introduced, but with less
than the full seating density. It is still too early to make any
definitive assessment of its impact on costs and fares.

**When jet aircraft replaced piston engine aircraft in the
1950's, their much lower operating cost per seat was

The Economist, commenting on this rather strange approach, states:

> An increase is even harder to justify when it is
> timed to run during the period in which the first jumbo
> jets are coming into service, with costs nominally
> a third below those of today's best aircraft. Even if
> the full savings are not realized straight off, either
> because fewer seats are installed than the aircraft
> can hold, or for technical reasons, they must still
> have the effect of holding costs down rather than put-
> ting them up . . . .
> Some of the proposals that have been tabled in
> the last five weeks at Cannes were quite openly for
> imposing a 10 to 15 percent surcharge on the big jets
> not because this was needed to cover their costs, but
> because they would otherwise look too comfortable to
> passengers tired of being cramped in today's 34-inch
> tourist seats (International Air Transport Associa-
> tion regulations prescribe the size) . . . . The sur-
> charge proposal looks like having been finally killed,
> because it was unlikely to get American (and one
> would hope also British) government approval. But
> the rather more sensible suggestion, that jumbos
> carrying the maximum seats (490 on a Boeing 747)
> should be allowed to charge less than those with fewer
> seats because they were (a) less comfortable and (b)
> cheaper to operate, got killed too . . . .
> . . . The rule that all fares must be unanimous
> tends to make IATA move at the speed of the slowest
> member and the handful of big airlines that used to
> act as a ginger group seem in the years of prosperity
> to have lost their bite. It is no excuse to argue, as
> airlines sometimes do, that air fares have risen
> much more slowly than other prices, and in real
> terms have fallen sharply. In a rapidly advancing
> technology this is just what one would expect. [2]

To this it should be added that, as earlier noted, the
carriage of cargo by aircraft is increasing rapidly and, with

counterbalanced by much excess capacity so that some airlines experienced financial difficulties and resisted fare cuts.
See Lucille S. Keyes, "The Making of International Air Fares
and the Prospects for their Control," Journal of Air Law and
Commerce, 30:177-8, 1964.

the introduction of the jumbo aircraft, which are well adaptable to all-cargo service, the thinking of airlines and governments should be directed toward attracting whole new categories of cargo traffic to air transport. Only in this manner can the interests of the world economy be properly served.

It would seem that the situation both as to passenger and cargo rates needs to be severely shaken in some manner so that the narrowly conceived prosperity of the airlines will be subordinated to the demands of the world economy and of the world public interest. The principal need is a changed philosophy but, insofar as the various systems of international regulation are concerned, it is the 1946 Draft which, by reason of its appellate body of international experts with rate powers, offers hope of assisting in the process.

One possible variant on any of the systems being discussed herein would be to substitute for the International Air Transport Association a body of governmental (rather than airline) rate experts, perhaps attached to the International Civil Aviation Organization. In a recently published work, Dr. K. G. J. Pillai proposes just such direct rate making by an intergovernmental body. [3]

Yet, because of the extreme complexity of world rate making, it would be likely that, where now airline officials sit about the table at traffic conferences, governmental representatives would sit at the table accompanied by the same airline rate experts. The practical difference between such a governmental body and the present International Air Transport Association could thus prove more apparent than real, especially when it is considered that--(1) most airlines are governmental corporations, albeit ordinarily separate from the governmental ministry of civil aviation or transportation, (2) IATA decisions must now be approved by the governments, although admittedly the latitude of this governmental power is limited by its having to be applied on a "package" of rates already agreed to by the airlines, and (3) the policies of airlines will often also be the policies of their governments--e. g., the preservation and promotion of the national airline may be a motive of its government every bit as much as it is a motive of the airline itself.

Nevertheless, it might be that the transfer of the basic rate conference function from the International Air Transport Association to such a body of government representatives would tend to shift the pressures within the elaborate network of negotiations to some degree toward world consumer interests and away from narrowly conceived airline interests.

The Welfare of the Less Developed Countries

Where this study would ask that the advanced industrial nations set aside as obsolete their considerations of national pride in having and promoting a "flag" carrier, it would ask rather the opposite with respect to the less developed countries. For such countries, there seems a psychological as well as an economic need to seek new endeavors, and, as was pointed out in Chapter 4, a service function such as operating an airline may lend itself well to the societies and economies of such states. The problems of obtaining sufficient traffic and of winning the confidence of travelers may indeed be great ones, but they need not deter a less developed country from making the attempt nor prevent the world community from viewing with sympathy the possible advantages to such countries of selling the world this service.

In particular, it should be recognized that technological innovations in an LDC tend to breed further innovations, if only to the extent that they tend to wake up the population and set people's minds into channels where their curiosity is aroused and they begin to think more in terms of changing their lives. It would seem that a national airline would have this effect every bit as much as a steel mill or an automobile factory.

Any system premised on bilateral route negotiations would appear to place most LDCs at a handicap. This is particularly true of the new African republics. An advanced industrialized country may well attach very little value to having its airline or airlines serve an African point. It, therefore, will lack the usual motive of reciprocity for permitting the African country to establish its airline in such service.

The presence in any system of the Bermuda principles as to frequency, capacity, and Fifth Freedom rights also involves a handicap for the LDCs, including those which have important traffic points, such as India and Brazil. As noted earlier, the traveling public, usually predominantly persons from the advanced countries, will tend to favor the airlines of their own and similar countries, and the LDC airlines will be the ones with the empty seats. Thus, countries with substantial airlines, such as India, Brazil, Mexico, and Argentina, have been particularly reluctant to accept all of the Bermuda system, especially with respect to Fifth Freedom.

Mexico, in its aviation relations with the United States, is an example. For many years, air services between the

two countries were authorized on a tentative basis without
the security of a bilateral agreement, in light of Mexico's
refusal to allow American air carriers the broad latitudes of
the Bermuda principles, and the American refusal to accept
an agreement without them. In 1957, however, the United
States prevailed and an agreement was executed on Bermuda
lines. Between that date and 1965, United States carriers
expanded their services greatly and won the major part of
the market. The Mexican airlines suffered disastrous losses
to the point where the Mexican Government began to exercise
frequency and capacity control over the United States airlines
despite the terms of the bilateral agreement. Finally, in
1965, the United States accepted limitations on its airlines'
frequencies on a temporary basis, but with specified increases
by steps at future dates. [4]

It will also be recalled from Chapter 2 that it was Mexico
which pressed, at the Geneva Conference in 1947, for a provision whereby a bilateral agreement could be executed granting no right whatever to carry Fifth Freedom traffic. The
vote to adopt the Mexican proposal involved largely the support of the countries which, in later years, were to be called
LDCs.

The Canadian and 1946 Drafts are rated "good" in Table
3 with respect to the interests of the LDCs. In the case of
the Canadian, an LDC could unilaterally establish at least a
token service of one flight a week to any point, with a right
to escalate later as traffic developed. The Canadian Draft
permitted carriage of Fifth Freedom traffic, but would have
limited the justification of capacity on the assumption that
Fifth Freedom equals one half of Third Freedom; this would
not be the ideal arrangement for the LDCs but it would place
at least some limitation on the major airlines operating far
from their home countries.

The 1946 Draft would permit unilateral establishment of
routes, but would use the Bermuda principles. The latter,
however, would not have the deleterious effect they often have
on the LDC airlines because (1) the frequency and capacity
provisions would be subject to the oversight of an international
regulatory body, and (2) the Fifth Freedom provisions would
depart from the Bermuda principles to the extent that a rate
differential might be used.

The 1947 Majority Draft is rated only "fair" since, although it would permit unilateral establishment of a route,
it would place the operation of the route under the Bermuda
language with no international regulatory body to oversee its

application and no provision for a rate differential for Fifth
Freedom.

The Geneva Draft is also rated "fair," since, though it
would involve the great disadvantages for the LDCs of bilateral route negotiations and the Bermuda language, it would
(as amended at Geneva by the Mexican provision above described) allow an LDC to seek bilateral agreements which
excluded or limited the carriage of Fifth Freedom traffic.
It will be recalled that at Geneva the LDCs were prepared
to accept the Draft with the Mexican amendment, and it was
the refusal of the other countries to accept the amended
Draft which caused the breakdown of that conference.

The 1947 Minority Draft, and the present system, are
rated "poor" since each involves the disadvantages to the
LDCs of bilateral negotiations, the Bermuda language, and
the absence of any control by an international regulatory
body.[*]

Contribution to World Peace

It is difficult to evaluate the impact of international cooperation in the economic regulation of the world's airlines
on such large matters as the reduction of international tensions and the promotion of a safer and more humane world
political system than exists today. Airline service is only
one of many facets of the problem, and it would be possible
to have a peaceful, humane world order wherein the economic
regulation of the airlines would still be under the present
system. Conversely, it would be possible to establish a high
degree of international cooperation, including a truly effective
world regulatory body, for the airlines, and at the same time
have the world political situation deteriorate. Clearly, the
questions with which this study is concerned will most certainly not, by themselves, be the determinants of world peace.

Yet it seems strange indeed, in light of the overwhelming
dangers in the current world political system, that governments should be so absorbed in such minor hazards as the

---

[*]The 1947 Draft and all the other systems have provisions for advisory opinions by the ICAO Council, arbitration
of disputes, or, in the case of the Geneva Draft, use of the
International Court of Justice. Those measures for ultimate
settlement of disputes are, of course, to be distinguished
from an international body of aviation experts performing
day-to-day regulatory tasks.

increased competition that their airlines might face from a
change in the regulatory picture. It would seem, instead, to
be the rational policy to take each of the numerous fields of
international administration, of which aviation is but one,
and seek to use each as a vehicle for the reduction of international tensions and the building up of machinery for the
practice of international cooperation. Such cooperation, to
the degree possible, should extend to the actual making of
decisions premised on the general public interest of the world
rather than of one's own country.

From this standpoint, the present system must be rated
"poor." As has been noted, the establishment of routes begins from what is tantamount to an embargo, and proceeds
via a bilateral bargaining process, with only IATA to serve
as an example of machinery of international cooperation in
the picture.

The Canadian and 1946 Drafts are rated "good" because
each would establish a multilateral route exchange doing away
altogether with the bilateral system and, in addition, would
establish an international regulatory body. There could, of
course, be disagreements among airlines and their governments, and even major grievances, under a multilateral
system of any sort. However, under the Canadian and 1946
Drafts there would be a really effective third-party judgment
such as is basic to any system of law, replacing a system of
bilateral dickering where the settlement is based on the relative power of the bargainers. What might be called a "due
process of law," or at least a step toward it, would thus be
established.

It is also well, in measuring the value of an effective
multilateral system, to consider the impact on the habits of
thought of the people involved, such as airline and government
officials and the traveling public, from a day-to-day awareness
that world airline service is governed (at least on an appellate
level) by an international body. Since, in the last analysis,
world peace requires the development of a sense of world
community among individual human beings, this type of psychological effect should not be neglected; it would receive a
beneficial impetus from the Canadian Draft and an even better
one from the 1946 Draft.

The 1947 Majority Draft is rated "fair" since it would
take one of the important steps found in the Canadian and 1946
Drafts, but not the other--i.e., it would scrap the bilateral
system in favor of a multilateral exchange of routes but would
not establish any international regulatory body.

The 1947 Minority and the Geneva Drafts are both rated
"poor" since both would retain the bilateral system and neither
would provide for any regulatory body. As will be noted later,
however, each of these two instruments should be given a
slender edge over the present system with respect to the promotion of world cooperation inasmuch as each would take a
small step toward multilateralism, albeit limited to the pre-
scribing for all bilateral agreements a uniform code of capacity and Fifth Freedom principles.

Implementation of the Best System

Since this study holds that the 1946 Draft is the preferable of the several systems, it appears desirable to discuss
briefly how a system of this or a similar type might be
brought into effect.

The basic instrument would be a multilateral treaty
negotiated at an international conference called by the Assembly of ICAO. In all likelihood, such a treaty would parallel
rather than supersede the Chicago Convention and would establish a regulatory body independent of ICAO, although a close
working relationship with ICAO in such matters as the exchange of information and statistics would be desirable. As
an administrative convenience, the body might well be located
at the seat of ICAO in Montreal, perhaps even in the same
building.

There are strong considerations favoring the separation
of the economic regulatory body from ICAO. Not all the
members of ICAO could be expected to accept the multilateral
convention. Perhaps the best that could be hoped for would
be that a nucleus of some of the countries in the western world
would ratify such a treaty and introduce among themselves its
international economic regulatory system, and that in subsequent years an example of an effectively operating system
would attract into membership other Western nations and
conceivably some day the Communist countries. Yet it is
important that ICAO be as near to a universal world body as
possible, partly because of its status as a specialized agency
of the United Nations, but also for the practical reason that
its navigation and safety functions make it highly desirable
that every country in the world through which international
airline service will pass should be a member. Safety and
navigation matters are less politicized than economic, as
the whole history of international aviation since 1944 (or even
since the 1919 Paris Convention) demonstrates. It appears

essential that ICAO not be reconstituted into a body covering both the safety/navigation and the economic spheres of regulation where such a combination would involve the exclusion from ICAO of a number of countries who would be unwilling to accept the multilateral economic arrangement.

The possibility must be considered of some degree of conflict between the extensive economic functions of the international regulatory body and those functions of ICAO bearing upon economics. The latter, however, consist merely of the making of studies and recommendations, and the gathering and publishing of statistics. Thus, the work of the ICAO economic personnel should be of help to the regulatory body rather than in conflict with it.

The question of obtaining acceptance of a multilateral treaty along the lines of the 1946 Draft is a difficult one. Certain countries, notably the United States, perhaps would have to be assured in the language of the treaty that the question of whether an airline should be privately owned or a government corporation would continue to be a matter within the sole discretion of each government and that there would be no requirement that a country limit itself to a single "chosen instrument" airline. Very likely the treaty would require that the international board honor what in American legal parlance are known as "grandfather rights," meaning that existing airlines would continue to exercise current rights over their existing routes under capacity and Fifth Freedom principles no less liberal than those now in effect.

In light of the difficulties which international political bodies such as the Security Council and General Assembly of the United Nations have had in giving practical effect to their actions in the political field, it may well be asked by what method an international regulatory body would compel obedience to its orders. The usual problem of the absence of an international police arm to execute the orders of an international body arises at once. Yet the solution is suggested immediately by the current experience of ICAO in setting navigation and safety standards, as well as by the experience of other international bodies such as the setting of international sanitary standards by the World Health Organization and of radio frequency allocations by the International Telecommunication Union. Briefly, the governments undertake when they ratify the pertinent treaty to enforce within their own jurisdictions the acts of the international body.

Thus, for example, the Federal Communications Commission of the United States requires that American radio

transmitters be operated within the radio frequency allocations
of the International Telecommunication Union. The refusal of
an American station to obey a proper order of the commission
would result in enforcement action backed by the courts of the
United States, including, if necessary, civil and criminal
penalties. Similarly, airlines, whether American or foreign,
while being operated in the United States, are subject to safety
and navigation procedures established by ICAO but enforced
by the Federal Aviation Administration backed by the courts
of the United States.

It may be asked how a signatory government could be
compelled to carry out an order of the international body if
it chose to refuse to do so. Were it possible for a government
to disobey with impunity any order it found displeasing, the
regulatory body might find itself in the powerless position in
which the United Nations has often found itself in dealing with
political questions such as Rhodesia, South Africa, or the
Arab-Israel dispute.

But there are pressures on governments in technical,
specialized fields of international cooperation where the
political element is relatively minor and the practical need
for international cooperation is great. A government disre-
gards a safety standard of ICAO at the risk of jeopardizing
the safety of its own aircraft and citizens as well as, in an
extreme case, actually cutting itself off from air communications with other countries if its airports and airways became unsafe due to refusal to abide by an internationally accepted procedure. Moreover, any responsible government
will hesitate to breach even a minor standard of ICAO (or
similar bodies such as the two mentioned above: the International Telecommunication Union and the World Health Organization) lest such an action weaken by its bad example the
delicate structure of cooperation established by treaty from
which each nation derives a thing of substantial value--good
international airline service, protection from radio interference, protection from the transmission of communicable
diseases, etc.

It is this knowledge within each government of the ultimate value of the system of international cooperation that is
the real factor inducing obedience to the international body.

The question remains whether governments would perceive such an ultimate value in a system of international economic regulation of world airlines, so that they would enforce
its orders even when contrary to the interests of their own
airlines. In this connection the 1946 Draft has an important

advantage: the body it would establish would not issue day-to-
day orders, but would merely be an appeal board when carriers and governments could not agree among themselves as
to rates or as to the applicability of the Bermuda frequency,
capacity, and Fifth Freedom principles. Orders would presumably be infrequent, and much accommodation of conflicting interests would occur outside the international regulatory
body.

A Second-Best System

What are the chances of obtaining agreement of the
governments to adopt the 1946 Draft or a similar instrument?
It would be necessary to arouse enthusiasm once again for
multilateralism, reversing the prevailing tendency to dismiss
as futile any idea of progress toward such a goal.

Yet this may be less difficult than might at first appear.
The period of over twenty years since the Geneva Conference
has seen an extraordinary growth in both passenger and cargo
traffic, and thus in the importance of world airline service,
as well as a great increase in the number of states having, or
desiring to have, their own airlines over world routes. The
conclusions (or lack of conclusions) reached in the 1944-47
era need not be governing in the minds of men who are con-
fronted today with this wellnigh geometric progression in the
size and complexity of the world airline system which they
are continuing to control under what indeed seems a nine-
teenth-century system of governance.

Nevertheless, the historical record in the more than two
decades since Geneva is certainly not encouraging to a pro-
ponent of multilateralism. Even the experience with respect
to intra-European services, described in Chapter 3, has
certainly been disappointing; neither Western Europe, under
the Council of Europe, nor even the six Common Market
countries despite their extremely close economic links, have
achieved any degree of multilateralism save the limited experiment with nonscheduled services.

Given both the absence of any significant achievement in
over two decades and the prevalence throughout that time of
a feeling of futility concerning the goal of multilateralism,
it would seem that to advocate the 1946 Draft today is to seek
the ideal rather than the attainable. It would be difficult
enough to persuade governments to abolish their bilateral
control over routes, but to this must be added the difficulty

of winning acceptance of a regulatory body such as the proposed ICATB.

Each of these steps would doubtless be thought of by many governments as involving a "surrender of sovereignty" in the sense of giving up both the right to say what airlines may serve one's country and the ultimate right to determine capacity and rate questions. This would, of course, not be a correct use of the term "sovereignty" since there would be no permanent, irrevocable transfer of these national prerogatives but merely their concession by treaty, an action common to many treaties, subject to the right of each state to take back its prerogatives by denunciation on a year's notice. Nevertheless, considering the strength of nationalistic sentiment, the idea of surrendering important aspects of one's country's powers would arouse opposition to any attempt to enact the 1946 or a similar Draft. Note, however, that with respect to the merchant marine, as pointed out in Chapter 1, the comparable rights have been generally relinquished by the nations of the world, by both treaty and custom.

A similar degree of opposition would also be aroused by the Canadian Draft, since it also involves the surrender of the same two national prerogatives.

Another reason for setting aside the 1946 (or the Canadian) Draft is that the chances seem remote indeed of obtaining the acceptance of such systems by the Soviet Union and China. ("China" as used hereinafter will refer to Communist China. The Chinese Nationalist Government on Formosa currently occupies the "China" seat in ICAO but, since it does not govern mainland China, it is not of much significance to world aviation.) It is important to bring both of these countries into any world regulatory arrangement in view of the great geographic area they occupy, athwart such important natural air routes as that between Europe and Japan.

The Soviet Union is by far the more important state of the two with respect to world aviation because of its much higher level of technological development. Its airline, Aeroflot, already has substantial international services which the Soviet Government is expanding into a worldwide network. Its presence in the bodies at Montreal working on problems of navigation and safety is highly advantageous for the obvious reason that its airline is using the world's airways and airports and, conversely, the airlines of other countries in increasing numbers are being permitted to fly into the Soviet Union. In addition, Soviet-manufactured civil aircraft are being sold more and more on the world market, and the acceptance of world safety standards in each detail of their manufacture is vital.

The U.S.S.R. can, of course, be part of the world system of navigation while at the same time remaining outside
any multilateral economic regulatory scheme. Yet, if one
considers that questions of capacity, Fifth Freedom, and
rates are essentially competitive, it appears difficult to conceive of a multilateral system working well with a major
competitor such as Aeroflot outside it.

The delegation of authority to the ICATB envisaged in the
1946 Draft would very likely be totally unacceptable to the
U.S.S.R. in light of its historic emphasis on its prerogatives
as a sovereign state, evidenced, among other things, by its
resistance to delegations of authority within the United Nations;
and it must be kept in mind that the Communist countries feel,
with some justification, that they are outnumbered and out-
voted in any universal international organization. *

Also, from the sheer standpoint alone of the promotion
of world peace, it appears highly important to have the Soviet
Union belong to any multilateral system in any field of human
endeavor. Thus, to advocate the 1946 Draft, with the likelihood that the Soviet Union would not accept it, would seem
unwise indeed.

It seems, then, that attention should be turned to a second
choice. The selection would appear to narrow to two very
similar instruments--that of the 1947 Minority and that of
the Geneva Conference. As will be seen by reference back
to Table 2, both would leave route negotiations on a bilateral
basis and would apply the Bermuda principles, with the same
rate-making system as today and no international regulatory
body.

The 1947 Minority Draft has the provision that a state in
a bilateral negotiation may decline to grant a route on only
one permissible ground--an "insufficiency of traffic." It is
not clear from the Draft whether the traffic in question is
that being carried by airlines already operating over the
route, or what it may be predicted that the additional airline
would carry. Nor is it clear how traffic is to be estimated

---

*The agreement between the United States and the Soviet
Union to permit airline service between New York and Moscow
(and even the Soviet Union's subsequent membership in the
ICAO, as of November 14, 1970) was not only the result of
prolonged negotiations but, as finally accepted, does not contain the Bermuda principles, nor need Aeroflot participate in
IATA or accept its rates. Instead, frequencies, capacity,
and rates are predetermined by the two governments.

when a route is requested over which there is no current airline service. Furthermore, there is no definition for the
subjective term "insufficiency," nor is there any assurance
that a state would not allege the "insufficiency" reason when
it had other motives for denying a requested route.

Yet the application of this language to bilateral route
negotiations would have certain advantages. It would tend to
set a philosophical basis for negotiations which might have at
least a persuasive effect on the governments. The philosophy
would outlaw, or at least drive underground, such motivations
as an equitable exchange of economic benefits which is the
basis today for grant of a route in American aviation policy.

In short, the language proposed in the 1947 Minority
Draft, if respected by the various states, might tend, in a
practical sense, to yield the benefits of the multilateral route
exchange envisaged in the Canadian, 1946, and 1947 Majority
Drafts, while maintaining the mechanics of bilateral negotiations. In fact, many of the provisions of those drafts were
seeking the objective of permitting an airline to establish
scheduled service where it wished (subject only to the consent
of its own government) provided that the traffic (or at least
the Third/Fourth Freedom traffic with some allowance for
Fifth Freedom) in the various markets was sufficient to support the new, along with the existing, service. The reasoning is quite rational from the standpoint of economics. Moreover, it is the basic reasoning behind decisions of the Civil
Aeronautics Board of the United States in regulating the domestic airlines. To seek to avoid an overproliferation of
airlines in a market seems a reasonable policy that serves
the world public interest, and, although it might be preferable to have the difficult questions of judgment weighed by an
international regulatory body, it is certainly better than
nothing to have the obligation placed upon the governments to
make such a policy the governing factor in bilateral route
negotiations.

Doubtless there would be instances where a government,
refused a route in a bilateral negotiation on grounds of "insufficiency of traffic," would disagree with the conclusion.
A form of third-party settlement of a dispute of this sort
would presumably be available, however, under the 1947
Minority Draft since it apparently would have included the
same provisions for third-party settlement as were in the
Majority Draft--i.e., the ICAO Council would have been empowered to establish an arbitral tribunal to resolve a dispute,

with the parties obligated to carry out the decisions of the
tribunal. *

An arbitral tribunal may well seem an unwieldy way to
resolve a question of "insufficiency of traffic" in a market,
and it might well prove difficult for such a body to make the
necessary determination since the question is an economic
rather than a legal one and would involve also a businessman's
judgment on such points as customer habits. The complain-
ant state might well allege that the addition of its airline to
the service in the market would attract new traffic rather
than divert it from existing services, or might allege other
controversial projections as to future traffic.

Yet it might well be that with these very problems in
mind, the President of the ICAO Council would select experts
in airline economics to serve on the tribunal. And it must
also be considered that not every grievance would go to arbitration; in the give-and-take of negotiation, the fact that a
state had the right to request arbitration might serve to cause
the other state to concede a doubtful point.

The Geneva Draft, by contrast, states flatly that: "No
Contracting State shall be required to enter into a Route
Agreement for the grant of such privileges."[5] In another
respect, too, it is disadvantageous by comparison with the
1947 Minority Draft: it provides for compulsory third-party
settlement of disputes only if they fall under Article 36, Section 2, of the Statute of the International Court of Justice,
whereupon they are submitted to that court. There are arbitration provisions also, but they are voluntary. It seems
scarcely likely that questions of capacity, Fifth Freedom,
and rates, involving as they do the intricacies of airline
economics, would lend themselves to the rather ponderous
juridical mechanism of the International Court of Justice.

While in the two foregoing respects the 1947 Minority
Draft appears the superior document, the Geneva Draft as
amended in the manner proposed by Mexico would appear to
offer a protection which many small countries, and in particular the LDCs, would feel that they need. It will be recalled
that at Geneva an amendment to the draft was adopted on
Mexico's motion, with support coming primarily from the
LDCs, whereby a bilateral agreement would be permitted
wherein the two states would deny each other any rights to
carriage of Fifth Freedom traffic.

---

*The Minority Draft consisted merely of a redrafting
of certain controversial articles in the Majority Draft, not
including those relative to settlement of disputes.

Perhaps few countries would take advantage of such an exception since it would involve a sacrifice for each country of its own airline's needs for fill-up traffic along the routes. More likely the Mexican amendment would be used as a basis for bilateral agreements which, instead of prohibiting Fifth Freedom traffic altogether, would permit it under circumstances far more restrictive than under the Bermuda language. In any event, inclusion of the language of the amendment in a proposed multilateral agreement might greatly increase the chances of obtaining approval of the agreement by the LDCs.

In light of all the foregoing, then, perhaps the best system to propose as a "second choice" to the more far-reaching Canadian and 1946 Drafts is the 1947 Minority Draft with its Bermuda Fifth Freedom provisions amended by the Mexican language picked up from the Geneva Draft. This would mean, in substance, that two countries could agree to limit or prohibit Fifth Freedom traffic vis-à-vis one another.

In any event, either the 1947 Minority or the Geneva Draft offers distinct advantages over the present system, though each retains the bilateral system. First, either Draft offers simplification, since, though there would continue to be a monumentally large number of bilateral agreements, there would be far fewer inconsistencies among them. True, under the Mexican amendment, some bilaterals might restrict or prohibit Fifth Freedom. But, as noted above, countries with long-range airlines would not wish to see them deprived of fill-up traffic and this fact would militate against seeking Fifth Freedom limitations.

The second advantage would be simply that the adoption of any multilateral agreement, even one as limited as the two being discussed here, might over time ease the various fears of the different nations as to the harmful effects on their airlines of any degree of international cooperation, and might open the way at some future date to acceptance of a true world regulatory system such as was proposed in the 1946 Draft. If nothing else were achieved, it might well be worth having even so relatively timid an adventure into multilateralism in order to revive world interest in the spirit that moved the nations back in the 1940's to plan and work toward a rational economic regulation of the world's airlines.

Lastly, any steps toward multilateralism, toward broadening man's experience with international administration, even such limited steps as here, would make at least a small contribution toward reducing international tensions. As noted previously, it would seem that, in light of the

transcendent importance of an improvement in the world
political situation, even a token increase in world cooperation
in one limited sphere is not a consideration to be lightly dismissed.

THE NEED FOR A CHANGE IN PHILOSOPHY

It has previously been stated, in the discussion above of
IATA and rate making, that much could be achieved without
a change in the system if only the philosophy of the governments could be altered. Conversely, no change in the mechanism can achieve a desirable rationalization of world airline
service unless governments acquire the will to pursue such
objectives. Whatever the particular problem, it is necessary
that governments place less emphasis on the protection and
development of their national carriers and more upon the
totality of international airline service as an asset that governments collectively hold in trust for the benefit of the peoples
of the world.
    The prevailing philosophy in the United States makes an
illustrative case, and here the problem is compounded by
what can only be described as a lack of candor. The following
is an excerpt from the official, public report of the Civil Aeronautics Board to the United States Congress for Fiscal Year
1968:

        Not all countries have subscribed to our econom-
    ic views of freedom in the marketplace of internation-
    al air transportation. In our relations with some
    countries, with and without benefit of a bilateral air
    transport agreement, we are, and have been, con-
    fronted with national policies of protectionism and
    restrictionism. They have usually taken the form of
    limits on capacity to protect the homeland carrier.[6]

The economic views of the United States most certainly
do not include "freedom in the marketplace of international
air transportation." To the contrary, the United States is a
strong supporter of the bilateral system with its implicit embargo on foreign airline service subject to bargaining for a
reciprocal exchange of benefits. Thus, it seems that the
United States pursues the very course that the above statement attributes to presumably less enlightened nations--i.e.,

"national policies of protectionism and restrictionism"--wherever such policies are considered advantageous to the American carriers.

A resemblance to other phases of American general commercial policy can be seen. Since the Reciprocal Trade Agreements program began in 1934, the United States has held itself forth as a champion of free trade, yet has not hesitated, and does not today hesitate, to use not only high tariffs but actual embargoes to block the consequences of free trade when such consequences would be particularly unpleasant. Examples are current quotas on imports of petroleum and certain dairy and meat products, as well as programs whereby foreign cotton textiles and steel are placed under a "voluntary" restraint on their export to the United States under threat of congressional action to make more difficult, or prevent altogether, the flow of this traffic. [7]

It is not the purpose of the present study to say whether some, or even all, of these trade restrictions are justifiable, but merely to point out that any assumption that the United States is a champion of free trade per se is not justified.

Perhaps what is needed throughout the international economic philosophy of the United States is a retreat from what may all along have been an unwarranted moralistic assumption--i.e., that free trade is necessarily virtuous and protectionism or restrictionism necessarily evil. Such thinking was a natural outgrowth of the world history of the 1920's and 1930's where barriers to trade, growing competitively higher and higher, tended to injure the world economy, to aggravate and slow recovery from the Depression, and indeed to bear a share of the blame for the rise of the Nazi movement and World War II.

Today, in light of the increased attention upon the LDCs, there is a growing belief that protectionism may achieve worthwhile purposes under certain limited circumstances, often depending on the particular country and its social and economic problems. The economic philosophy of the Prebisch school, discussed earlier, is illustrative. Another economist who has written forcefully along this line is Gunnar Myrdal, who describes the results of unlimited free trade as, in effect, the rich getting richer and the poor poorer. [8]

In the field of international aviation, it is particularly inappropriate to use "restrictionism" and "protectionism" as pejorative terms since airline service by its nature requires economic regulation for its very existence, whether this be by an international regulatory body, as advocated herein, or by the present system of elaborate airline and governmental interactions.

What is being suggested here is a reorientation of philosophy which might be broken down very roughly into the following three objectives: (1) an excellent world airline system, featuring particularly a substantial reduction in rates, premised on the concept of a world system at the service of the peoples of the world and the economy of the world; (2) departures from the previous objective to the extent made necessary by the excruciatingly difficult economic, social, and psychological problems of the LDCs; (3) the development of mechanisms of international administration not only in pursuit of the previous two objectives but for their own sake, that is to say, as a step toward reduction in international tension and the promotion of world peace.

There has been a general absence of an international outlook in governments, as can be illustrated by nothing more than the fact that the multilateral concept was, in 1947, allowed virtually to perish, and, at this writing, shows no signs of revival. To achieve a broader world philosophy will require that many men within the airlines and governments extend themselves to look beyond the traditional shibboleths of aviation policy.

In this connection, Inis Claude, describing the negotiation of a multilateral treaty as a quasi-legislative process resembling "congressional maneuvering to synthesize numerous interests," concludes that the "most pressing requirement" in such a process is "internationally-oriented leadership."[9]

One thing seems clear: the use (and thus the social and economic significance) of international airline service will continue rapidly to increase, perhaps to a degree beyond what can now even be imagined. The situation seems clearly to call for a more enlightened philosophy than has thus far prevailed respecting its economic regulation.

NOTES

1. This thought was expressed by Dr. Urban G. Whitaker, Jr. in a talk at American University on May 13, 1969.

2. "Air Fares: Surely They're not Serious," The Economist, (October 19, 1968), p. 90.

3. A. G. J. Pillai, The Air Net (New York: Grossman Publishers, 1969), pp. 129, 134. Dr. Pillai also suggests, as an alternative, that a body of experts be appointed by ICAO to make continuing studies of airline fares on behalf of world consumer interests, receive complaints from consumers and governments, and participate in IATA meetings.

4. H. Max Healey, "Revisions to the Mexico-United States Air Transport Agreement, 1965-1970," Journal of Air Law and Commerce, 32:167-94, 1966.

5. ICAO Document 5230, p. 136.

6. Civil Aeronautics Board Reports to Congress-- Fiscal Year 1968 (Washington: Government Printing Office, 1968), p. 131.

7. See, for example, news items in The Wall Street Journal, (January 7 and March 3, 1969); Editorials in The Wall Street Journal, (January 13 and 15, 1969).

8. Gunnar Myrdal, Rich Lands and Poor (New York: Harper and Bros., 1957), pp. 3-7, 11-12, and 143-57.

9. Inis L. Claude, Jr., "Multilateralism--Diplomatic and Otherwise," International Organization, 12:43-52, 1958.

APPENDIXES

A

The provisions relative to capacity and Fifth Freedom contained in the below-quoted paragraph 6 of the "Bermuda Agreement" (United States-United Kingdom Air Transport Services Agreement of 1946) have come to be known as the "Bermuda principles" and have been incorporated (with some variations) in numerous bilateral agreements.

(6) That is is the understanding of both Governments that services provided by a designated air carrier under the Agreement and its Annex shall retain as their primary objective the provision of capacity adequate to the traffic demands between the country of which such air carrier is a national and the country of ultimate destination of the traffic. The right to embark or disembark on such services international traffic destined for and coming from third countries at a point or points on the routes specified in the Annex to the Agreement shall be applied in accordance with the general principles of orderly development to which both Governments subscribe and shall be subject to the general principle that capacity should be related: (a) to traffic requirements between the country of origin and the countries of destination; (b) to the requirements of through airline operation; (c) to the traffic requirements of the area through which the airline passes after taking account of local and regional services.

The 1946 Draft grants all Five Freedoms, without need for bilateral route negotiations, but limits routes to those "constituting reasonably direct lines" to the foreign country from the home country of the airline. The capacity language is that of Bermuda with some minor differences. A rate differential may, however, be imposed making the rate for a Fifth Freedom passenger as much as 10 percent higher than for a Third/Fourth Freedom passenger over the same segment. The differential might be even higher than 10 percent if the International Civil Air Transport Board found this inadequate to protect airlines exercising Third/Fourth Freedom rights from destructive competition by airlines exercising Fifth Freedom rights. Rates could be initiated by an airline, an airline conference, or a state. A state objecting to a rate would consult the other state; if they could not agree, the matter would be referred to the International Civil Air Transport Board.

Article 15. Airlines shall have "reasonable discretion" regarding initial capacity, but each government must keep its airlines from "unduly continuing to operate excessive capacity" or "initiating capacity obviously in excess of requirements and intended for destructively competitive purposes."

Article 20. "Rates shall be deemed unreasonable if they are found by the board to depart unduly from the level indicated by the costs of the most economic comparable operator, plus a profit reasonable in the circumstances."

Article 27. An International Civil Air Transport Board

is established, consisting of from five to seven members, to be elected by the Assembly of ICAO. The exact number of members, their terms of office, and compensation are to be determined "from time to time by the Assembly."

Article 28. "The board shall interpret and administer the provisions of this agreement."

Article 29. An "aggrieved" state may ask the board to investigate "and order the corrective action necessary." But the grievances are limited to: (1) inadequacy of a Fifth Freedom rate differential, or hardship resulting from one, (2) "operation or threatened operation of excessive capacity by airlines," (3) unreasonably high or low rates, and (4) unfair competitive practices or unfair subsidies.

Article 31. Only a state may be a party to a board proceeding. Any board decision may be appealed within thirty days to the ICAO Council.

Article 32. The ICAO Council may dismiss, void, or affirm the board's decision, or refer it back to the board for further proceedings.

Article 33. All parties "shall conform" to the board's decisions and shall require their airlines to conform. Otherwise, the board "shall certify the failure to the Council" which "may, thereupon, in its discretion": (1) "authorize or require" any state to prohibit the operation in its air space of the airline or airlines of a state that is not conforming to the board decision, or (2) recommend to the ICAO Assembly that such a state "be suspended from any or all of its rights and privileges under this agreement." The Assembly may enact such suspension by a two-thirds vote.

Article 35. The board may hold hearings, conducted by one board member or by hearing examiners, but the whole board must hear arguments on request of any party, and "all decisions shall be rendered by the board."

Article 36. Each government "agrees to make available to the board and its representatives any information (other than information classified as secret or confidential for reasons of national defense) reasonably required for the proper discharge of the board's duties, and to require its nationals to do likewise upon the request of the board."

Article 41. After the agreement has been in effect for one year, any state may denounce it on a year's notice.

Article 6. Subject to the provisions of this Agreement, each Contracting State shall have the right that its duly authorized airlines shall be entitled to fly their aircraft across the territory of any other Contracting State without landing and to make, in such territory, stops for non-traffic purposes and for the purpose of putting down and taking on passengers, mail and cargo.

Article 8. Any Contracting State desiring to exercise the rights conferred by Article 6 of this Agreement shall give four months' prior notice to each other Contracting State in whose territory it intends its international air service to land and one month's prior notice to each other Contracting State over whose territory it intends its air service to operate without landing. . .

If the government of any State receiving such notice considers that the operation of the proposed air service is inconsistent with this Agreement or with the Convention, it shall, as soon as practicable, so advise the State which gave the notice. Should disagreement between the two States result, it shall be dealt with as provided in Article 17 . . .

Each Contracting State shall require its airlines to keep the aeronautical authorities of other States advised as to the frequency of its operations, the time-table to be followed, the types of aircraft to be used, and other relevant operating data.

The giving of the notices and other information called for by the foregoing provisions of this article is the only formality which may be required of any Contracting State as a condition precedent to the exercise of the rights conferred by this Agreement.

Article 10. (a) The amount of capacity which a Contracting State shall be entitled to permit any of its airlines to provide from time to time over various stages of each route shall be that required for the carriage, at a reasonable load factor, of both:

(i) passengers, mail and cargo taken on or to be put down by such airline in the territory of such State; and

(ii) passengers, mail and cargo moving by such airline between points in the territories of other States which the route touches, insofar as capacity for such traffic is not being provided by airlines of the States in which such traffic is taken on or put down . . .

Article 11. Any Contracting State may permit its airlines reasonable discretion as regards the amount of capacity to be offered on the initiation of now international air services.

Article 12. Article 10 shall not be interpreted to require changes in capacity more frequently nor at a larger number of points along a route than is consistent with sound operating practices of through international air services.

Article 13. Nothing in this Agreement shall prevent unfilled capacity in any aircraft operated under this Agreement. from being used for the carriage of any passengers, mail and cargo offered.

Article 14. Each Contracting State shall require that its airlines charge reasonable rates. Such rates may be set by airlines or by the respective Contracting States in which they are established. If any Contracting State considers rates charged by an airline of another Contracting State to be unreasonable and injurious to it, and if a disagreement results, such disagreement shall be dealt with as provided in Article 17.

Article 15. Each Contracting State shall refrain from granting to airlines any form of assistance which fosters competitive practices destructive to other airlines.

Article 17. (a) Any disagreement arising between Contracting States on the interpretation or application of this Agreement, which cannot be settled by negotiation, shall be resolved by an arbitral tribunal, the members of which shall be appointed by the President of the Council of the International Civil Aviation Organization. The method of selecting members of such arbitral tribunal and the conduct of their proceedings shall be governed by rules as established by the Council.

(b) If, upon the application of any Contracting State as to a matter covered by Article 8 or Article 14 of this Agreement, the President of the Council of the International Civil Aviation Organization, on evidence submitted, shall be of the opinion that a temporary restraining order is required, he may issue such order. The order of the President shall remain in effect until the decision of the arbitral tribunal comes into force, unless sooner modified or revoked by him prior to that event.

(c) Contracting States shall conform to decisions of such tribunal and orders of the President, and shall require their airlines to conform thereto. If an airline of any Contracting State fails to conform to any such decision or order, each other Contracting State undertakes not to allow the operation of such airline through the air space above its territory, until such time as the airline is acting in conformity to such decision or order.

Article 21. (a) Contracting States may give notice of their denunciation of this Agreement, not less than one year after its coming into force, to the Secretary General of the International Civil Aviation Organization. Such denunciation shall take effect one year from the date of the receipt of the notification . . . .

D

Article 7. (a) The right of any Contracting State under
this Agreement to land aircraft in the territory of any other
Contracting State for the purpose of putting down and taking
on passengers, mail and cargo shall be given effect through
separate arrangements to be made between the competent
aeronautical authorities of such States concerning the routes
to be flown between and beyond their respective territories,
and the airports of entry and points to be served in their
respective territories.

(b) In designating routes to be followed and airports to be
used, pursuant to this Agreement and to Article 63 of the Convention, the following principles shall be observed:

(i) Each route shall constitute as nearly a direct course
out from and back to the territory of the State whose nationality the aircraft possesses as may be consistent with the
requirements of the traffic originating and terminating in such
State;

(ii) There shall be a fair and equal opportunity for the
carriers of the respective States to operate air services on
the agreed routes between their respective territories.

(iii) No Contracting State shall decline an exchange of
routes with any other Contracting State on any grounds other
than an insufficiency of traffic to justify the proposed operations, or otherwise discriminate unfairly against any such
State . . .

Article 10. (a) The services provided by any airline of
a Contracting State, over any air route arranged under this
Agreement shall bear a close relationship to the requirements

of the public for such transport and shall have as their primary objective the provision at a reasonable load factor of capacity adequate to the current and reasonably anticipated requirements for the carriage of passengers, mail and cargo taken on or to be put down in the territory of such State.

(b) Provision for the carriage of passengers, mail and cargo moving between points in the territories of other States which any such route touches shall be made in accordance with the general principles that capacity shall be related to:

(i) traffic requirements between the country whose nationality the airline possesses and the countries of destination of the traffic;

(ii) requirements of through airline operation for fill-up traffic; and

(iii) traffic requirements of the area through which the airline passes after taking account of other air transport services established by airlines of the States concerned.

Article 8. The privileges granted to a Contracting State of taking on and putting down international air traffic in the territory of another Contracting State under the provisions of the present Agreement shall be granted only by a separate arrangement (hereinafter called a Route Agreement) between such Contracting States. No Contracting State shall be required to enter into a Route Agreement for the grant of such privileges.

Article 9. Nothing in the present Agreement shall prevent a Contracting State from entering into a route agreement which will grant to another Contracting State only the privilege of taking on and putting down international air traffic originating in or destined for the territory of the other party to the Route Agreement, and not the privilege of carrying international air traffic both originating in and destined for points on the agreed routes in the territories of States other than the parties to the Route Agreement.

Article 15 . . . . (i) The air services provided by a designated airline under a route agreement shall have as their primary objective the provision, at a reasonable load factor, of capacity adequate to the current and reasonably anticipated requirements of that airline for the carriage of international air traffic originating in or destined for the territory of the party designating the airline;

(ii) The capacity provided under Sub-paragraph (i) may be augmented by complementary capacity adequate for the carriage of international air traffic both originating at and destined for points on the agreed routes in the territories of

States other than that designating the airline. Such additional complementary capacity shall be related to the traffic requirements of the areas through which the airline operates, after taking account of the special position of other air services established by airlines of the States referred to above, insofar as they are carrying, on the whole or part of the agreed routes, international air traffic originating in or destined for their territories . . . .

Article 16. In the development of long distance air transport services to meet the needs of the public for such transport, the development of local and regional services shall not be unduly prejudiced. Subject to the other provisions of the present Agreement, it is recognized that the development of such local and regional services is a primary right of the Contracting States concerned.

Article 18. (a) The rates to be charged for passengers and freight on any international air services operated under route agreements shall be fixed at reasonable levels. Due regard shall be paid to all relevant factors, including costs of operation, reasonable profit and the rates charged by other airlines on any part of the route.

(b) The rates shall be agreed, if possible between the airlines, in accordance with one of the following alternatives:

(i) Through such rate resolutions as may be adopted by an organization representative of airlines (hereinafter called the airlines' organization), accepted for that purpose by the Contracting States concerned; or

(ii) Where no such organization is available, between the airlines of all Contracting States which operate over the route or any part thereof.

(c) Any agreement made pursuant to Paragraph (b) shall be transmitted to the Contracting States whose territories are served by the route or whose airlines exercise traffic rights thereon (hereinafter called the Contracting States concerned) and to the Organization. Such agreements may become effective two months after receipt thereof by the Contracting States concerned unless one or more of such Contracting States have given notice of disapproval to the Organization. The Organization shall immediately give notice of such disapproval to the Contracting States concerned.

[The remainder of Article 18 sets forth elaborate procedures in the event of intergovernmental disputes over rates, including consultations and referrals to the International Court of Justice or an arbitral tribunal.]

Article 21. (a) If any dispute arises between Contracting States with respect to the interpretation or application of the present Agreement, or of a route agreement concluded hereunder, they shall use their best efforts to settle such dispute by negotiation.

(b) If such dispute cannot be settled by negotiation, and it is a dispute within the subjects stated in Article 36 (2) of the Statute of the Court, it shall, upon the request of any party to such dispute, be referred for decision to the Court. The Contracting States hereby declare that they accept the jurisdiction of the Court and will comply with its decision, and with any provisional measures which ought to be taken to preserve the respective rights of the parties indicated by the Court pending its final decision in respect of any dispute to which they are parties and which is referred to the Court under this paragraph.

(c) Contracting States that are parties to a dispute may in the alternative, if they so agree, refer such dispute for final decision to an arbitral tribunal composed in accordance with Article 22 or to some other person or body. The Contracting States agree that the decision of such arbitral tribunal or other person or body, and any provisional measures indicated by it pending its final decision, shall be binding on the parties to such dispute.

[Article 22 provides for a panel of experts from which can be drawn the arbitral tribunals referred to in Article 21.]

[Article 31 allows denunciation on a year's notice at any time at least two years after entry into force of the Agreement.]

BIBLIOGRAPHY

BOOKS

Arne, Sigrid. United Nations Primer. New York: Farrar
& Rinehart, Inc. , 1945.

Acher, Robert K. , et al. The United Nations and Promotion
of the General Welfare. Washington: The Brookings
Institution, 1957.

Caves, Richard E. Air Transport and its Regulators.
Cambridge: Harvard University Press, 1962.

Cheng, Bin. The Law of International Air Transport. London:
Stevens & Sons, 1962.

Charington, Paul W. Airline Price Policy. Boston: Harvard
University Press, 1958.

Claude, Inis L. , Jr. Swords Into Plowshares. Third edition.
New York: Random House, 1964.

Cooper, John C. The Right To Fly. New York: Henry Holt
& Co. , 1947.

Corbett, David. Politics and the Airlines. London: George
Allen and Unwin, 1965.

Daggett, Stuart. Principles of Inland Transportation. Third
edition. New York: Harper and Bros. , 1941.

Das-Gupta, A. K. Planning and Economic Growth. London:
George Allen and Unwin, 1965.

Fair, Marvin L. and Ernest W. Williams, Jr. Economics
of Transportation. Second edition. New York: Harper
and Brothers, 1959.

Frederick, John H. Commercial Air Transportation. Fourth
edition. Homewood, Illinois: Richard D. Irwin, Inc. ,
1955.

Fulbright, J. William The Arrogance of Power. New York: Random House, 1966.

Gill, Frederick W. and Gilbert L. Bates. Airline Competition. Boston: Harvard University Press, 1949.

Goedhuis, D. Idea and Interest in International Aviation. The Hague: Martinus Nijhoff, 1947.

Haefele, Edwin T. Transport and National Goals. Washington: The Brookings Institution, 1969.

Keyes, Lucille. Federal Control of Entry into Air Transportation. Cambridge: Harvard University Press, 1951.

Lissitzyn, Oliver J. International Air Transport and National Policy. New York: Council on Foreign Relations, 1942.

McDougal, Myres S. , Harold D. Lasswell, and Ivan A. Vlasic. Law and Public Order in Space. New Haven: Yale University Press, 1963.

McWhinney, Edward and Martin A. Bradley. The Freedom of the Air. Dobbs Ferry, N. Y. : Oceana Publications, 1968.

Myrdal, Gunnar. Rich Lands and Poor. New York: Harper and Bros. , 1957.

Ogburn, William F. The Social Effects of Aviation. Boston: Houghton Mifflin Co. , 1946.

Pegrum, Dudley F. Transportation: Economics and Public Policy. Homewood, Illinois: Richard D. Irwin, Inc. , 1963.

Pillai, K. G. J. The Air Net. New York: Grossman Publishers, 1969.

Richmond, Samuel B. Regulation and Competition in Air Transportation. New York: Columbia University Press, 1961.

Schenkman, Jacob. International Civil Aviation Organization. Geneva: Librairie E. Droz, 1955.

Smith, Henry L. Airways Abroad. Madison: University of Wisconsin Press, 1950.

Straszheim, Mahlon R. The International Airline Industry. Washington: The Brookings Institution, 1969.

Thayer, Frederick C., Jr. Air Transport Policy and National Security. Chapel Hill: University of North Carolina Press, 1965.

Thomas, Aaron J. Economic Regulation of Scheduled Air Transport, National and International. Buffalo: Dennis, 1951.

Wassenbergh, H. A. Post-War International Civil Aviation Policy and the Law of the Air. The Hague: Martinus Nijhoff, 1962.

Wheatcroft, Stephen. Air Transport Policy. London: Michael Joseph, 1964.

_____. The Economics of European Air Transport. Cambridge: Harvard University Press, 1956.

Wright, Quincy, ed. The World Community. Chicago: University of Chicago Press, 1948.

PUBLICATIONS OF GOVERNMENTS, INTERNATIONAL ORGANIZATIONS, AND LEARNED SOCIETIES

Cooper, John C. "International Ownership and Operation of World Air Transport Services." Document for use at the Second Edwin G. Baetjer Memorial Conference, Princeton University, 1946. (Mimeographed.)

European Economic Community. Treaty Establishing the European Economic Community. Brussels: Publishing Services of the European Communities, 1961.

International Air Transport Association. World Air Transport Statistics. Montreal: International Air Transport Association, 1967.

International Civil Aviation Organization. Documents 5230, 7017, 7148, 7225, 7278, 7409, 7415, 7417, 7456, 7676, 7695, 7799, and 8185. Montreal: International Civil Aviation Organization, 1947-61.

_____. European Civil Aviation Conference Working Papers 1/WP/2, 1/WP/61, and 5/WP/45. Montreal: International Civil Aviation Organization, 1955, 1964.

Prebisch, Raul. Towards a New Trade Policy for Development. New York: United Nations, 1964.

Provisional International Civil Aviation Organization. Documents 1577, 2089, and 4014. Montreal: Provisional International Civil Aviation Organization, 1946-7.

_____. PICAO Journal. Montreal: Provisional International Civil Aviation Organization, 1946.

Stanford Institute. Air Transport Development and Coordination in Latin America. Washington: Organization of American States, 1961.

United Nations. Statistical Yearbook. New York: United Nations, 1967.

United States Air Coordinating Committee. Report of the Air Coordinating Committee on Civil Air Policy. Washington: Government Printing Office, 1954.

United States Civil Aeronautics Board. Handbook of Airline Statistics. Washington: Government Printing Office, 1967.

United States Civil Aeronautics Board. Civil Aeronautics Board Reports. Vol. VII. Washington: Government Printing Office, 1948.

United States Civil Aeronautics Board. Reports to Congress-- Fiscal Year 1968. Washington: Government Printing Office, 1968.

United States Department of State. Foreign Relations of the United States, 1944. Vol. II. Washington: Government Printing Office, 1967.

United States Department of State. Proceedings of the International Civil Aviation Conference. 2 Vols. Washington:
Government Printing Office, 1948.

United States Department of State. Treaties and other International Acts. No. 1507. Washington: Government
Printing Office, 1946.

United States Department of Transportation. Press Release
17-S-69, June 5, 1969.

The White House. "Statement on International Air Transport
Policy." Washington: The White House, April 24, 1963.
(Mimeographed.)

PERIODICALS

"Air Fares: Surely They're Not Serious," The Economist,
October 19-25, 1968, p. 90.

"The Air After Chicago," The Economist, December 30, 1944,
pp. 860-2.

Air Transport World, October, 1968, pp. 50-2; January, 1969,
p. 29; February, 1969, pp. 21-4.

Asher, Robert E. "U.N. Aid to the U.S.," International
Development, II:15-9, June, 1965.

Aviation Week and Space Technology, March 10, 1969, pp.
179-84.

"Can Air Union Get Airborne?," The Economist, August 4,
1962, p. 459.

Claude, Inis, Jr. "Multilateralism--Diplomatic and Otherwise," International Organization, 12:43-52, Winter,
1958.

Constantin, James A. "Multilateralism in International
Aviation," Southern Economic Journal, 16:197-209,
October, 1949.

Cooper, John C. "Some Historic Phases of British International Civil Aviation Policy," International Affairs,
23:189-201, April, 1947.

"European Civil Aviation Conference," Journal of Air Law
and Commerce, 28:78-94, Winter, 1961.

Gazdik, J. G. "Conference on the Co-ordination of Air Transport in Europe--Strasbourg--April 21-May 8, 1954,"
Journal of Air Law and Commerce, 21:330-8, Fall, 1954.

Goedhuis, D. "Questions of Public International Air Law,"
Recueil des Cours, 81:201-305, 1952.

_____. "The Role of Air Transport in European Integra-
tion," Journal of Air Law and Commerce, 24:273-85,
1957.

Hackford, R. R. "Our International Aviation Policy,"
Harvard Business Review, 25:483-500, 1947.

Healey, H. Max. "Revisions to the Mexico-United States
Air Transport Agreement, 1965-1970," Journal of Air
Law and Commerce, 32:167-94, 1966.

Heymann, Hans, Jr. "The Soviet Role in Civil Aviation,"
Journal of Air Law and Commerce, 25:265-80, 1958.

Johnson, G. Griffith. "The International Aviation Policy of
the United States," Journal of Air Law and Commerce,
29:366-71, 1963.

Keyes, Lucille B. "The Making of International Air Fares
and the Prospects for Their Control," Journal of Air
Law and Commerce, 30:173-92, 1964.

Koffler, Warren W. "IATA: Its Legal Structure--A Critical
Review," Journal of Air Law and Commerce, 32:222-35,
1966.

Larsen, Paul B. "The United States--Italy Air Transport
Arbitration," American Journal of International Law.
61:496-520, 1967.

Little, Virginia. "Control of International Air Transport,"
International Organization, 3:29-40, February, 1949.

Lissitzyn, Oliver J. "Bilateral Agreements on Air Transport," Journal of Air Law and Commerce, 30:248-63, 1964.

_____. "International Aspects of Air Transport in American Law," Journal of Air Law and Commerce, 33:86-101, 1967.

Macrae, Norman. "No Christ on the Andes," The Economist, October 1, 1965, (Unnumbered special insert section.)

Mankiewicz, Rene H. "Aircraft Operated by International Operating Agencies," Journal of Air Law and Commerce, 31:304-10, 1965.

McClellan, Grant S. "British and United States Air Policies Shaped by Postwar Trade Goals," Foreign Policy Bulletin, 24:2-3, November 17, 1944.

Official Airline Guide, February and April, 1969.

Padwa, David J. "The Curriculum of IMCO," International Organization, 14:524-47, 1960.

Pouroalet, Michel. "The International Element in Air Transportation," Journal of Air Law and Commerce, 33:75-85, 1967.

Prebisch, Raul. "Commercial Policy in the Underdeveloped Countries," American Economic Review, 49:251-73, May, 1959.

Sackrey, Charles M., Jr. "Overcapacity in the United States International Air Transport Industry," Journal of Air Law and Commerce, 32:24-93, 1966.

Soviet Life, August, 1967, pp. 36-9.

Stabenow, Wolfgang. "The International Factors in Air Transport under the Treaty Establishing the European Economic Community," Journal of Air Law and Commerce, 33:117-31, 1967.

Stoffel, Albert W. "American Bilateral Air Transport Agreements on the Threshold of the Jet Transport Age," Journal of Air Law and Commerce, 26:119-36, 1959.

Thomas, Ivor. "Civil Aviation--International Questions Outstanding," International Affairs, 25:56-65, 1949.

"Three Airlines Are Better Than Two," The Economist, May
3-9, 1969, pp. 59-60.

Travel Weekly, May 27, 1969, p. 21, and June 10, 1969, pp.
25-32.

Wold, Edward M. "ICAO and the Major Problems of International Air Transport," Journal of Air Law and Commerce, 20:454-62, 1953.

Wold, Edward M. "Some Notes on the Multilateral Agreement
on Commercial Rights of Non-scheduled Air Services in
Europe," Journal of Air Law and Commerce, 23:180-7,
1956.

Van Zandt, J. Parker. "The Chicago Civil Aviation Conference," Foreign Policy Reports, 20:291-6, February 15,
1945.

Warner, Edward. "The Chicago Air Conference: Accomplish-
ments and Unfinished Business," Foreign Affairs, 23:406-
21, April, 1945.

UNPUBLISHED MATERIALS

Hackford, R. R. "The International Aviation Policy of the
United States." Unpublished Doctoral dissertation,
Harvard University, 1948.

Nelson, Robert A. "Scandinavian Airlines System: A Case
of International Cooperation." Unpublished Doctoral
dissertation, Clark University, 1954.

Strom, Harold K. "The North Atlantic Air Transport Market--
A Study of the American Competitive Position." Unpublished Doctoral dissertation, University of California
at Los Angeles, 1964.

Weibel, Eugene A. "International Civil Aviation and Federal
Power." Unpublished Doctoral dissertation, Harvard
University, 1962.

NEWSPAPERS

New York Times, September 6, 1964.

Wall Street Journal, January 7, 13, 15, and March 3, 1969.

INDEX

William E. O'Connor has served as a Foreign Affairs Officer in the Department of State and subsequently as a Foreign Affairs Analyst in a division of the Civil Aeronautics Board responsible for negotiation of air transport agreements and for consultations with other governments relative to airline problems. He is presently Assistant Chief of a division responsible, among other things, for the international charter services of both United States and foreign airlines.

Dr. O'Connor was graduated from Brown University, received his Master's degree in Foreign Affairs from George Washington University in Washington, D. C., and in 1970 received his doctorate in International Studies from the American University, also in Washington.

DATE DUE

18